THE BURGUNDIAN CODE

University of Pennsylvania Press
MIDDLE AGES SERIES
Edited by Edward Peters
Henry Charles Lea Professor
of Medieval History
University of Pennsylvania

A listing of the available books in this series
appears at the back of this volume

The Burgundian Code

BOOK OF CONSTITUTIONS
OR LAW OF GUNDOBAD

ADDITIONAL ENACTMENTS

Translated by

KATHERINE FISCHER DREW

Foreword by

EDWARD PETERS

Copyright © 1949, 1976 by the University of Pennsylvania Press

Foreword copyright © 1972 by
the University of Pennsylvania Press, Inc.

Library of Congress Catalog Card Number: 70-182499

5th paperback printing 1996

ISBN 0-8122-1035-2

Printed in the United States of America

FOREWORD TO THE
PENNSYLVANIA PAPERBACK EDITION

Edward Peters

THE great frontier which divided the inhabitants of the Roman Empire from the Celtic and Germanic peoples who lived beyond their northern provinces consisted not only of forts, frontier settlements, and defense works, but of cultural and institutional differences as well. To the Romans, these people were *barbari,* barbarians who did not know the life of the city nor the gifts of literacy. Although Germans often settled within the imperial frontiers, joined the Roman army—eventually coming to command it—and even served the diplomatic interests of the Empire outside its borders by waging war with tribes who were still its enemies, the persistent Roman attitude toward the barbarians remained a powerful force until the disappearance of the Roman Empire in the West in the fifth and sixth centuries. Yet from the second century, that frontier was subtly transformed. Germanic military tactics altered the traditional Roman military structure; Germanic costume appeared frequently in Roman fashion; ultimately entire Germanic peoples were absorbed by the Empire, either through diplomatic negotiation or by invasion from outside. The proximity of Roman institutions, of course, altered the structure of Germanic society even more rapidly than the Germans influenced the Romans. Roman forms of military command and provincial administration, Roman agricultural and social institutions, and the Latin language itself produced irreversible changes among those barbarians who eventually inherited the western part of the Roman Empire and became the first Europeans.

In no area is the transformation of the frontier between German and Roman more apparent than in the appearance of the law codes of the Germanic peoples from the early fifth century on. The very act of writing down Germanic customary law was a triumph of Roman influence, and its consequences continue to influence the legal structures of much of the world down to the present day. Professor Drew's translation of the *Liber Constitutionum sive lex Gundobada* and the *Constitutiones Extravagantes* constitutes *The Burgundian Code,* a Germanic lawbook compiled by the Burgundian kings Gundobad and Sigismund in the last quarter of the fifth century and the first quarter of the sixth. This translation gives the reader of history a portrayal of the social institutions of a Germanic people far richer and more exhaustive than any other available source. This work is important not only for historians of legal institutions, but for social historians and anthropologists as well. In the last few years there has been renewed interest in these early Germanic law codes as evidence for a broad range of problems in the history of human society. Professor Drew's translation and introduction of *The Burgundian Code* should contribute to that interest and broaden the appeal of these law codes to a wider range of social and cultural investigations than they have traditionally been associated with.

Since the original publication of this work in 1949, a number of other works have appeared in English which enhance the importance of Professor Drew's work and constitute a useful body of literature for further research. The work of anthropologists and the points at which their own research into the social structure of primitive societies touches early medieval law has recently been summarized by Max Gluckmann in his *Politics, Law, and Ritual in Tribal Society* (New York, paper, 1968). Professor Drew herself has studied the role of the barbarian kings in the shaping of these law codes in a number of studies, most comprehensively in "Barbarian Kings as Lawgivers and Judges," an article in Robert S. Hoyt, ed., *Life and Thought in the Early Middle Ages* (Minneapolis, 1967), pp. 7–29. The collected papers of Floyd Seward Lear, published as *Treason in Roman and Germanic Law* (Austin, Tex., 1965), deal with a wider range of topics than the title indicates and are indispensible for further study in this field. Paul Vinogradoff, *Roman Law in Medieval Europe* (3rd ed., Oxford, 1961) offers the best short study of the relationship between Roman and Germanic laws now available in English.

The reprinting of Professor Drew's translation of *The Burgun-dian Code* ought therefore to appeal to a much wider range of readers than simply those concerned with legal history. Those social institutions reflected in the law codes of the Germanic peoples illuminate not only the differences between Roman and barbarian, but those between underdeveloped and developed societies, and between the stages in the history of a society itself in which transformations of the utmost importance can only be traced, not in written histories or memoirs, but through the new forms of expression which the transformation takes. A society's conception of precisely what law is—and, by implication, what it is not—is a much-neglected but valuable indicator of the character of that society itself. Professor Drew has enabled the English-speaking reader to discover some of these aspects of Burgundian society at a crucial period in its history.

PREFACE

THE original suggestion for this translation of the Burgundian Code derives from the interest and appreciation in the early Germanic laws and institutions which Dr. Floyd Seyward Lear of the Rice Institute has incorporated in his various writings and instilled in the minds of his students. To him my greatest appreciation is extended for the careful and painstaking supervision which he gave both the original translation and subsequent revisions and for his help in guiding me through the difficult secondary materials in the field of early legal history.

Neglect of the barbarian codes in recent times is unfortunate, for they contain a large amount of material relating to the impact of barbarian custom upon Roman law. They give a detailed description of social habits and legal institutions resulting from that impact and provide a veritable mine of information regarding the functioning of barbarian society and its relationship to the Romans whom the barbarians conquered. The Burgundian Code is generally regarded as an extremely important barbarian code because of its comprehensive treatment of the laws of inheritance, of the division of property, and of the definition of social relationships in the Burgundian kingdom.

My thanks are due also to Mr. J. L. Battista of the Rice Institute for his assistance in determining the meanings of some of the more obscure Latin words and phrases. The publication of the Code in this series is due to the interest shown by Dr. John L. LaMonte of the University of Pennsylvania, whose suggestions proved of value in revising both text and introduction for publication.

KATHERINE FISCHER DREW

CONTENTS

Continuation of the Book of Constitutions

Constitutiones extravagantes
(Additional Enactments)

INTRODUCTION

1

The Burgundians were one of the East Germanic tribes. They first came into contact with the Roman Empire in the third century when they had established themselves just east of the Rhine along the Main River, where they and other groups of barbarians continually threatened the Roman frontier. For over a century longer the Romans were able to prevent the barbarian hordes from overrunning the Empire completely, but by the fifth century internal conditions within the Empire had so weakened it that the frontier garrisons and armies were no longer able or willing to maintain their defenses. In the year 406, when the attention of Rome was directed toward the Visigoths who had crossed the Balkan peninsula and were threatening Italy, the Vandals, together with the Alani, Suevi, and the Silingii, poured across the undefended Rhine frontier. Perhaps the Burgundians also intended to join this invasion. At any rate, by 413 they had appeared on the west side of the Rhine and had entered on a campaign against Roman upper Germany, conquering Worms, Speier, and Strassburg. Here in the region west of the Rhine, the center of which was the city of Worms, the Emperor Honorius gave them land, making the Burgundians *foederati* of the Roman Empire.

Lasting from about 413 until 436, this first Burgundian kingdom is the one of legendary fame, of the *Nibelungenlied* and *Waldhere* legends. It was overthrown by a Hunnish army in the employ of Rome in 436, at which time the Burgundian king, Gundahar, and a large number of Burgundians were killed.

Somewhat later the remnants of the Burgundian tribe were assigned territory in Sabaudia north of Lake Geneva by the Roman government. Here they became firmly enough established to be able to set up a second federate kingdom by 443 under the leadership of their king, Gundioc (437–74). From here the Burgundians

1

gradually extended their kingdom southward along the Rhone River. In 474 Gundobad, the son of Gundioc, became king of the Burgundians, perhaps sharing the kingship for a time with his two brothers, Godigisel and Chilperic. This Gundobad was king of the Burgundians from 474 to 516. Under his leadership, the Burgundian kingdom reached its greatest extent: to the northwest it extended as far as Langres; to the northeast to the northern Jura Mountains; to the east to the Alps; to the west it was bounded by a portion of the Rhone River and the upper course of the Loire; and for a time, the Burgundian kingdom also included Provence to the south, but this was soon lost to the Ostrogoths. Also under Gundobad, a codification of the Burgundian customary law was begun, and this work was completed by his son, Sigismund.

For a time the Burgundian kingdom was threatened by the stronger kingdom of the Visigoths to the west and south, but following the accession of Clovis as king of the Salian Franks in 481, the Franks rose rapidly in position and influence. Under the guise of furthering Catholic Christianity against the Arian Christianity of the Burgundians, Clovis attacked Gundobad in 500, but being unable to win a decisive victory over him, Clovis instead entered into an alliance with Gundobad against the Visigoths, and together they succeeded in winning a decisive victory over the Visigoths at Poitiers in 507.

In 516 Gundobad died and was succeeded by his son, Sigismund, who may have shared the rule with his brother Godomar. In 523 the Franks, now under the leadership of Clovis' sons— Chlodomir, Childebert, and Clothaire (Chlotar)—renewed their attacks against the Burgundian kingdom. Sigismund was killed, and a part of the Burgundian kingdom was lost while Sigismund's brother, Godomar, became king of the Burgundians. Godomar made repeated efforts to renew the strength of his kingdom, but the Franks were determined to have Burgundy. In 532 the Burgundians were defeated and Godomar driven into flight, and in 534 the Burgundian kingdom was divided among the Frankish rulers. This was the end of the second and the last independent Burgundian kingdom, although her local counts remained strong and from time to time became powerful enough to be able to rule almost independent of their Frankish and later Hapsburg rulers. The tradition of independence lived on in the region, and Burgundy as part of that much disputed Middle Kingdom was destined to play an important role throughout the Middle Ages.

2

When dealing with the barbarian codes, we are faced with the conflict between customary and statutory law. Customary law develops as the result of a mode of life over an extended period of time rather than as the result of a single legislative act whereby special enactments are set forth which are decreed to be binding on the people. This is not to say that customary law, even in its unwritten state, is not as binding upon the people as statutory law. The very fact that customary law has been built up as the result of a long process of development means that it is accepted as a standard of judgment because it has received the time-honored acceptance of the people and as such should be as strictly obeyed as any law decreed by an absolute ruler. Customary law (*mos*) is a body of moral practices established by the immemorial customs of a people and having a binding moral force rather than the arbitrarily enforced power of statutory law (*lex*), which is a body of specific statutes supported by a positive legal authority and guaranteed and enforced by political power. But even though *mos* is the broader and vaguer term, it is yet more fully obeyed than *lex*, for it has a moral force enhanced by social acceptance and as such cannot conscientiously be ignored as is often the case with regard to man-made law, which requires an agent of enforcement not contained in the conception alone that it is law.

Customary law is usually associated with personality of law—that is, the law by which a man should be judged is determined by his person, no matter where he happens to be at a given time. Statutory law, on the other hand, is usually associated with territoriality of law—that is, persons are to be judged according to the law in force in the territory in which they happen to be.

In the difference between customary law and statutory law lies the basic legal conflict between the barbarians and the Romans. The law that the Germans brought with them into the Empire was a body of unwritten custom, customs according to which they had lived for hundreds of years and which they regarded as personally binding. This body of custom was regarded as the inalienable possession of every individual German; no matter where he was, it was his right to be tried or to negotiate according to his own tribal law. When the Germans entered the Empire, their unwritten customary law associated with the individual German conflicted with the written statutory law of the Romans where the law was the same for all people within a certain territory. When the Germanic kingdoms were established within the Western Empire, the Germanic rulers encountered the problem of deciding by what law their Germanic and Roman subjects should be judged. Extending the personality of law principle, these Germanic rulers usually adopted a policy which permitted the Romans to be judged according to their own written Roman law, while the barbarians continued to be judged according to their own customs.

As the barbarian kingdoms became more firmly established, it became evident that laws for both Romans and barbarians must be defined more explicitly in order to be applied with any uniformity by the judges. Accordingly, there developed two kinds of written law in the barbarian kingdoms: the *leges romanae* for the Roman people, and the *leges barbarorum* for the Germanic people. The *leges romanae* were compiled from the works of the later Latin jurists and reflect a decline in Roman culture, a barbarization of the classic Roman law. The *leges barbarorum*, on the other hand, represented the writing down of the ancient Germanic customs as they had been influenced by Roman law, and this influence is reflected in the fact that all the barbarian codes (except that of the Anglo-Saxons) were written in Latin rather than in the native Germanic tongues.[1]

Burgundy, being a part of Gallia Narbonensis, had been subject to Roman law for centuries as a part of the Roman Empire. The Roman territorial law had been extended to the provincials here and was in general use at the time the Burgundians established themselves there in the fifth century. Because the Roman

[1] Harold Dexter Hazeltine, "Roman and Canon Law in the Middle Ages," *Cambridge Medieval History*, V, 720–21.

law had become so firmly established in this old Roman province, the coming of the Burgundians, who lived according to the unwritten traditions of their tribe, meant an even more radical collision between personal law and territorial law than in other regions of Gaul where the Roman population was neither so dense nor so firmly established. But the Burgundians had entered the valley of the Rhone peacefully, and perhaps even at the invitation of the Roman provincials who sought to enlist their military aid, so there was not much incentive for either people to enforce their laws or customs upon the other. Since the Burgundians were *foederati* of the Empire and as such entitled to a part of the lands before held entirely by the Romans, there was naturally much need of a code of law to govern commercial and social relations between the two peoples. The Burgundians were evidently willing to live up to the trust which the Gallo-Romans had put in them when they practically invited them to become their rulers, and we find that the Burgundians did not forcibly subject the Roman population of their kingdom to the Burgundian customary law, but rather they attempted to establish codes of law which would be fair to both Burgundians and Romans. *Leges barbarorum* were drawn up to govern relations between Burgundians, or between a Burgundian and a Roman; *leges romanae* were to govern relations between the Romans.

In the case of the Burgundians, the compilation of these laws for both the Burgundians and the Romans was undertaken by Gundobad, king of the Burgundians from 474–516. The lawbook for the Burgundians is known variously as *Lex Burgundionum, Liber Legum Gundobadi, Lex Gundobada, la Loi Gombette,* and *Gombata;* that for the Romans simply as the *Lex Romana Burgundionum* or, because of an early mistake in manuscripts, as the "Papian."

The dates of both of these books are not known definitely; however, the *Lex Romana Burgundionum* was probably written after the earlier part of the *Lex Gundobada.* The *Lex Romana Burgundionum* embraced criminal, private, and procedural law, but it was not intended to supplant all other Roman law then in use in Burgundy. It was intended as a supplementary instruction to the judges and not as a complete codification of the Roman law. Compiled under the leadership of Gundobad, the *Lex Romana Burgundionum* was based on the three *Codices*, the *Sententiae* of Paul, a writing by Gaius, and school interpretations. This law, however, did not remain influential for long because after the Frankish conquest of the Burgundians in 532 the *Breviary of Alaric*, which had been compiled by Alaric for the Roman subjects of his Visigothic kingdom, was used to enlarge or supplement the *Lex Romana Burgundionum*, and finally even replaced it.[2]

The *Lex Gundobada* has been transmitted in thirteen manuscripts, none of which are earlier than the ninth century. Five of these have a text of 105 titles, the remainder have 88 titles or add to them a varying number of supplements. The lawbook was evidently not all composed at the same time, and from internal evidence the first 88 titles seem to be older and form a more complete edition of the laws; Titles 88–105 and the *Constitutiones Extravagantes* seem to be later work supplementing various titles of the older lawbook—they are not completely different laws, but are additions merely defining the earlier laws more exactly. Authorities usually refer to these later titles as the *additamenta*, and they are generally accepted to be later additions to the book of laws by private individuals rather than the official declaration of the ruling monarch.

Although an earlier date has been suggested by some, the *Lex Gundobada* in a written systematic form probably reaches back no further than the reign of Gundobad, who came to the throne in 474. In fact, it is very unlikely that the earliest portion of the lawbook, Titles 2–41, was written down before the publication of the *Lex Visigothorum*, which was compiled in its earlier form in 483 under the leadership of Euric, then king of the Visigoths. This *Lex Visigothorum* probably served as some sort of model to Gundobad, as for instance, the prohibition against enforcing legal transactions which dated before the year 451: this time limit is marked by the Battle of Chalons in the Burgundian lawbook and by the death of Theodoric I, who fell in that battle against the Huns, in the Visigothic Code.

Some of the Titles 42–88 bear dates from 501 to 517 in varying order, those before 516 being the work of Gundobad, and those

[2] *Ibid.*, V, 722.

after 516 the work of his son, Sigismund. From the rhetorical style of writing and internal references to "earlier laws," it seems likely that none of this group dates before 501.

Because the name of the lawgiver differs from Gundobad to Sigismund in the preface of a number of the manuscripts, it has been held by some that these Burgundian laws went through a series of revisions, one or more being made by Gundobad, and one by Sigismund. However, this does not seem likely since the laws which are dated after 501 state that they are made to fit conditions not covered by the "earlier" law—they do not completely restate the law and supersede it as would have been the case if a revision had taken place. The preface was probably written by Sigismund since the statement that it was written in the second year of the reign of the king and issued from Lyons would probably make it too early to have been written by Gundobad, and also Gundobad's capital seat was at Vienne rather than at Lyons. Also, the style of the preface is more like that of Titles 42–88 than that of the earlier group. So the preface might have been composed and added at a time of reissuing the laws of Gundobad, when Sigismund had some of the later additions made.

Ignoring Title I which has definitely been revised, we may say, generally speaking, that the earlier part of the lawbook, Titles 2–41, was compiled sometime between 483 and 501; the second part, Titles 42–88, between 501 and 517; and the later part, Titles 89–105 and the *Constitutiones Extravagantes*, sometime during the reign of Godomar (524–32), or after the fall of the independent Burgundian kingdom.

It is fitting that this lawbook be called chiefly the work of Gundobad, for Gundobad had the longest rule of the Burgundian kings while the Burgundians held a federate kingdom, and under his leadership the country reached the height of its power and the limits of its territorial expansion. As a code of law, the *Lex Gundobada* was one of the most influential of the barbarian codes, for even after the Frankish conquest of the territory, the *Lex Gundobada* remained in force among the Burgundians and references are made to its use as late as the ninth century. The Burgundian Code is also important since it represents a transitional stage in the development of later European law. It reflects the earliest fusion of the Germanic and Roman law, for already in the Burgundian lawbook some of the typically Germanic elements are lacking—such as the assembly of freemen which played an important part in the government of the early Germanic tribes, and a system of fines and compositions has been substituted for the Germanic idea of the blood feud where the killing of a man obligated the members of his family to avenge his death upon the killer or upon his family.

3

As compiled by Gundobad, the *Lex Gundobada* probably did not represent the first attempt at the reduction to writing of the Burgundian customary law. Early in the fifth century, just after the Burgundians had entered the Empire in the wake of the larger migrations of the vandals and Franks, the Burgundians had been given land by Honorius and had set up a federate kingdom with its capital at Worms. Although nothing is known about this early Burgundian kingdom, their Germanic system of law must surely have come into conflict with the Roman law in force in this northern part of Gaul and have been influenced by it. This earlier kingdom was destroyed in 436, but by 443 the Burgundians had set up a new kingdom somewhat south of the first, and they were again established as *foederati* of the Empire. This meant that the Burgundians had had two experiences with the Roman system of land tenure and of provincial government. Surely a body of unwritten customs could not be stretched to furnish precedents for the establishment of themselves as guests upon a people who were already firmly settled and ruled by a comparatively complex system of law. So there must have been some attempt to write down certain of their laws before the time of Gundobad, and we do find references in the early laws of Gundobad which refer to earlier laws, laws which were not included in his version of the lawbook and which have not come down to us. For instance, in Title XVIII, 1, there is a law which states that it is replacing the "ancient rule of blame." This law provides that if the animals of one man injure the animals of another man, then the man whose animals caused the injury should turn them over to the man whose animals were injured—implying that under the "ancient rule of blame" a man was held accountable for the actions of his animals and would have to compensate for the injury in some way.[1] But nowhere is this "ancient rule" specifically stated.

It is possible that Gundobad had some of the laws written down before making an official collection of them. Since it is not likely that his official collection was published before 483 because of its relation to the Code of Euric,[2] this probably meant that there were a good many laws already in existence by the time the official collection was made. But not all these laws were included in the collection—laws which modified earlier laws seemed to take their place and the earlier law dropped out. Such for example seems to have occurred in the case of Title IV, 7. This law provides that if a horse is taken and ridden without the permission of its owner, then a composition must be made to the owner of the horse if it has been taken for a journey of one day only. The law further states "if indeed for more than that, let him (the thief) be held according to that law which we have ordered to be observed concerning horses used for journeys"—but the law referred to here does not exist in the lawbook as we have it.

To the original edition of Gundobad, later laws were added by Gundobad himself and by his son, Sigismund. The difference in style between the early work of Gundobad (Titles 2–41 as we now have them) and that of his later additions (*novellae*) indicates that these earlier laws were merely a writing down of usage which had already become established, for they are usually simple statements of the law. On the other hand, the *novellae* are

[1] See *Lex Gundobada*, XVIII, 1, n. 1.

[2] The *Lex Gundobada* is in close relationship with parts of the Code of Euric, for example, XVII, 1: "All cases which involve Burgundians and which were not completed before the Battle of Chalons are declared dismissed." The same time limit, the year 451, is set in the Code of Euric by a reference to the death of Theodoric I, the Visigothic ruler who fell in this battle. Other parts of the *Lex Gundobada* seem related to certain of the *leges antiquae* of the *Lex Visigothorum*, and also to the *Lex Baiuwariorum*, the *Lex Salica*, and the Lombard Edict, all of which came under Visigothic influence. For parallels of the Burgundian law with Visigothic, Lombard, Bavarian, and Salic laws, see H. Brunner, *Deutsche Rechtsgeschichte*, I, 505, n. 33.

more rhetorical, usually introduced by some generalized legal principle which often has little to do with the law itself as it follows.

Both the earlier laws (*antiquae*) and the *novellae* seek to govern the personal relations between individuals—all public law is lacking. The statement of the law is in legislative form entirely. It consists of rules of law rather than juristic opinions or cases serving as precedents. In one instance only is a definite case cited, its judgment to serve in the future as law. This is Title LII, the case of Aunegild, a widow, who after the death of her husband, became pledged to Fredegisil, the sword-bearer of the king; and Fredegisil accordingly paid the marriage price for her. Aunegild broke her pledged faith by an illegal union with Balthomodus, whereupon Aunegild was compelled to pay her price, three hundred solidi, to Fredegisil, and Balthomodus had to establish with witnesses that he was unaware of her pledged faith. The significant part of the law is the last paragraph: "In truth we command that the judgment set forth in this case be established to remain the law forever, and lest the moderation of the composition now permitted encourage anyone hereafter to commit a deed of such great crime, we command that whosoever incurs the guilt of such a deed not only may sustain the loss of his property, but also may be punished by the loss of his life." Thus, this case constitutes a rule of law and does not serve merely as a precedent.

In many respects the Burgundian legislation seems to be a body of tribal custom that has evolved considerable distance in the direction of positive statute law, especially in the case of the *novellae*. In its successive additions and modifications there can be seen a trend toward the establishment of a body of royal legislation; that is, rather simple customary rules have developed into a more complex royal legislation. Thus, the *Lex Gundobada* represents a trend away from tribal custom based on moral sanction to royal enactment based on the political authority and power of the king.

4

The barbarians who were allowed to enter the Empire as *foederati* were established on the land by a system of hospitality. This system was based on the old Roman precedent of quartering the soldiers on the land, allowing them one-third of the property of the original owner. The barbarians became acquainted with this system as a part of the Roman army because, in the days of its later weakness, the Empire had an army made up chiefly of barbarians.

The Germanic peoples originally came into collision with the Roman Empire because they were seeking land. They had reached the agricultural stage of civilization, and it was necessary for each barbarian to have a sizable piece of land for himself, for the barbarians knew nothing of concentrated life in cities. When it became evident that the Romans could no longer withhold the invading hordes, they entered into agreements with certain of the barbarian tribes—in Gaul, the Visigoths, Burgundians, and Salian Franks—whereby the barbarians were allowed to enter the Empire peacefully as *foederati* under an arrangement whereby they shared the land with the Roman inhabitants. In the provinces where barbarians had been settled in such a way, the Roman provincials usually outnumbered the barbarians, but, without an army, were subject to their rule. It is in this sense that the barbarians became *foederati:* they set up independent federate kingdoms, but these kingdoms were still considered within the Empire and as such received the nominal protection of Rome and in return agreed to defend their territories against other invaders.

The Burgundians had first entered into such an agreement with the Empire early in the fifth century, when they were given land by Honorius and set up a kingdom with its capital at Worms. Just what arrangement was followed in this early division of land we do not know, but it was probably the same as that followed after 443, when the Burgundians became *foederati* for a second time, setting up a kingdom in Sabaudia, the capital of which finally became Lyons. It is with the system of hospitality followed at the establishment of the kingdom in 443 that the *Lex Gundobada* indirectly deals.[1] The arrangement seems to have been that the

[1] The laws in the original edition of Gundobad which deal with the division of the land seem to be lacking. References in later laws (LIV, 1), providing that those who had not received lands from the largesse of the king might divide with a Roman host, may imply that the Burgundians were present in Sabaudia for a time before definite legislation concerning the division of land was enacted.

Burgundians were to receive two-thirds of the land and one-third of the slaves of the Roman with whom they had been assigned hospitality. The unusual division of two-thirds of the land and one-third of the slaves must have made a fairly equal division according to the Burgundians.[2] Since the Roman slaves were of relatively little use to the barbarian, it seemed more desirable to him that he have a larger amount of land. The land obtained by the Burgundian as the result of this allotment was designated *terra sortis* [3] and as such was regulated by rules of inheritance differing from those governing lands acquired by other means. In this manner, the Roman became the host (*hospes*) of the Burgundian, and the Burgundian became the guest (*hospes*) of the Roman.

The lands which the Burgundians obtained as a result of the division by lot were hereditarily owned and may have been subject to some sort of military service to the king, since the Burgundians as *foederati* of the Empire probably owed some military service to Rome in return for the recognition of their federate position within the Empire. However, even if the Burgundians in general did not owe military service in return for their *terra sortis,* those who held lands bestowed directly by the king as a reward for services rendered rather than land acquired at the general division do seem to have owed some sort of service to the king in return. That this is true seems to be implied by Title I, 4, which provides that the property of those who had received land from the king's grant should pass to their posterity if they served with such devotion and faith that the gifts of the king and his predecessors might be increased and preserved. In addition, those people who received land from the king were not allowed to acquire two-thirds of the land or one-third of the slaves from their Roman host (LIV, 1).

Generally speaking, the period of the Burgundian kingdom is too early for an evolved feudalism, but there certainly does seem to be an incipient feudal structure already appearing. In the first place, although the Burgundians had enjoyed only a relatively short period of development within the Roman Empire (from the

---

[2] This division is suggested by LIV, 1.
[3] I, 1—*terra sortis titulo acquisita.*

time they crossed the Rhine in 406 until 474, the accession of Gundobad), the power of the kingship seems to be definitely established. The king no longer seems to be only one among equals, as was true of the relation of the early Germanic kings to their nobles, but he seems to have become definitely the head of the state, both in time of peace and in time of war. The Burgundian nobles—and also some Roman nobles—referred to in the laws as *optimates*, evidently attended the king's council and rendered advice although there is no implication in the laws that the king did anything more than consult these counsellors, or that he felt himself bound to follow their advice when given. The *optimates*, in addition to their social position as being the highest class in the realm and their attendance at the king's council, seem to have had certain administrative duties, especially judicial. It is not clear whether all the *optimates* were judicial officers or not. Chief of the judicial officers were the counts of the cities and villages (*comites civitatum et comites pagorum*), under whom there were a number of other judicial officials designated simply as *judices*, about whom we know nothing as to how they were selected, their social position, or the remuneration which they received for their judicial duties. In the preface to the *Lex Gundobada*, there is also a reference to the *judices militantes* (Pref., 5) but there is no indication of their social position or to whom they were responsible. Since the superior position of the *optimates* seems to have been based upon their holdings in a given community, it seems likely (in view of their higher wergeld and the higher composition imposed in cases of crimes committed against them) that they enjoyed extensive holdings in the localities, in return for which they were in charge of the local administration of justice.

In the relation between the Burgundian "guest" and the Roman "host" we have a contractual relationship determined by law which may be a step in the development of the contractual feudal relationship between a lord and his vassal. In the case of the Burgundians and Romans, of course, the relationship is based on legal and social equality, but the fact that the Burgundians received two-thirds of the land and that the Burgundians were the stronger people physically would make it inevitable that the guest would assume some sort of superiority over his host, based upon economic and social differences in their position.

Another indication of the trend toward feudalism is the existence of a class of agricultural servants, *coloni* and *originarii.* Among the Burgundians the *coloni* and *originarii,* a group of people bound to the soil, seem to have been closer to the slave or unfree status than was true of the medieval serf who could not ordinarily be sold away from his land, but there is already a clear distinction between the slave and the *colonus,* for the *colonus* is fined rather than beaten in the case of a criminal act, and he seems to have enjoyed at least a semilegal competence.

The Burgundian kingdom is among the early Germanic kingdoms established within the Roman Empire, and yet the Burgundian Code reflects a marked degree of influence by the Roman law and customs. On the other hand, the presence of the Burgundians meant a definite breakdown of the old Roman system of social life and government. It is remarkable that the new system revealed by the Burgundian Code is as complete as it is after such a short period of development within the Roman Empire, and its completeness attests to the ability of the Burgundian kings and administrators in devising and administering a code of laws which would and did maintain harmonious relations between two such widely different peoples.

LIBER CONSTITUTIONUM
SIVE
LEX GUNDOBADA

BOOK OF CONSTITUTIONS
OR
LAW OF GUNDOBAD [1]

PREFACE

FIRST CONSTITUTION

1. In the name of God in the second year of the reign of our lord the most glorious king Gundobad, this book concerning laws past and present, and to be preserved throughout all future time, has been issued on the fourth day before the Kalends of April (March 29) at Lyons.[2]

[1] The text followed in this translation is that of L. R. deSalis, *Leges Burgundionum* (*Monumenta Germaniae Historica*, Sectio I, Tomus II, Pars I) (Hanover, 1892).

[2] The following is a translation of the Restored Introduction of the True Law of Gundobad as devised by DeSalis:

First Constitution

The most glorious Gundobad, king of the Burgundians. Since we have given deep thought to the enactments of our predecessors and of ourselves regarding the peace and welfare of our people, we have considered what is most fitting to promote honesty, discipline, good sense, and justice with reference to individual cases and titles of law. We have consulted on all these matters with the nobles (*obtimates*) of our people, and we have attempted to write down not only our own opinion but theirs as well, established in laws to last forever. For the love of justice through which God is pleased, etc.

This introduction as restored by DeSalis may represent the introduction prepared by Gundobad at his original collection of the laws, while that given in the main text may represent a preface prepared by Gundobad's son, Sigismund, at a later period when Sigismund reissued the lawbook together with additions of his own. That this is true is indicated by the fact that in Section 1, a number of the manuscripts designated by DeSalis A 1, 2, 3; B 1, 2, 4, 6, attribute the codification of this work to King Sigismund whose name is substituted for that of King Gundobad in this first section. Also, the fact that this preface was issued from Lyons would point to a period in Sigismund's reign since Gundobad ruled from Vienne while Sigismund ruled from Lyons. Manuscripts A 4; B 5, 7, 8, 9, 10, 11, retain the name of Gundobad. Cf. *ibid.*, pp. 29–30.

2. For the love of justice, through which God is pleased and the power of earthly kingdoms acquired, we have obtained the consent of our counts (*comites*) and leaders (*proceres*), and have desired to establish such laws that the integrity and equity of those judging may exclude all rewards and corruptions from themselves.

3. Therefore all administrators (*administrantes*) and judges must judge from the present time on between Burgundians and Romans according to our laws which have been set forth and corrected by a common method, to the end that no one may hope or presume to receive anything by way of reward or emolument from any party as the result of the suits or decisions; but let him whose case is deserving obtain justice and let the integrity of the judge alone suffice to accomplish this.

4. We believe the condition of this law should be imposed on us that no one may presume to tempt our integrity in any kind of case with favors or rewards; first, since our zeal for equity repudiates from ourselves those things which we forbid to all judges under our rule, let our treasury accept nothing more than has been established in the laws concerning the payment of fines.

5. Therefore let all nobles (*obtimates*), counsellors (*consiliarii*), bailiffs (*domestici*), mayors of our palace (*maiores domus nostrae*), chancellors (*cancellarii*),[3] counts (*comites*) of the cities or villages, Burgundian as well as Roman, and all appointed judges and military judges (*judices militantes*) know that nothing can be accepted in connection with those suits which have been acted upon or decided, and that nothing can be sought in the name of promise or reward from those litigating; nor can the parties (to the suit) be compelled by the judge to make a payment in order that they may receive anything (from their suit).

6. But if any of those mentioned, corrupted against our laws, or even judging justly, has been convicted of receiving rewards from suits or decisions, and the crime has been proved, let him be punished capitally as an example to all: with the further provision that the penalty which has been imposed shall not cause any loss of

[3] We have little information about the functions in the Burgundian kingdom of the various officials mentioned here in the preface. For *proceres* (Sec. 2), cf. DuCange, *Glossarium Mediae et Infimae Latinitatis*, V, 460; for *consiliarii*, cf. *ibid.*, II, 551; for *domestici*, cf. *ibid.*, II, 904; for *cancellarii*, cf. *ibid.*, II, 79–84; and for *notarii* (Sec. 7), cf. *ibid.*, IV, 647.

property to the sons or legitimate heirs of him whose dishonesty was punished.

7. Indeed for the payments given to the scribes (*notarii*) of our appointed judges in rendering decisions in suits exceeding ten solidi,[4] we give the opinion that a single tremissis should suffice;

[4] There are three Roman coins named in the Burgundian Code: the solidus, the semissis, and the tremissis. The solidus was a gold coin which under Constantine succeeded the aureus and continued to be coined until the fall of the Byzantine Empire. In western Europe it was later called the bezant. Originally, the solidus was worth about 25 denarii, although in the later empire it was reduced to about half that amount; as a medieval money of account it was equal to 12 denarii. The semissis was a coin minted under the later emperors worth half a solidus and said to contain 59.8 grains of gold. The tremissis was worth a third of a solidus. However, it is hard to give any comprehensible value to these moneys, even in purchasing power, since it would seem almost impossible for the Burgundians of the lower classes to raise the sums which might be levied against them under the terms of the laws. It has been suggested by Professor Summerfield Baldwin of the University of Akron that the establishment of a wergeld (money value) which was placed upon the life of each barbarian, a wergeld described in the laws in terms of Roman money, was an attempt by the barbarians to establish their social and legal equality with the Romans, to set some value upon their lives which might be comprehensible to their Roman subjects, a value which in the barbarian mind represented the inherent worth and dignity of a particular individual, yet also a value which was modified by his special class and position in society. In such a case the wergeld placed upon the life of a man or the composition set for stealing animals or inflicting certain wounds might not necessarily mean that the Burgundian kings meant an actual exchange of money to take place. Instead these values might indicate the relative value placed upon the lives of individuals of different classes, or they might indicate the importance set upon the stealing of certain animals or the inflicting of certain wounds in the minds of the barbarians since their more primitive revenges and compositions would hardly be accepted by their more advanced Roman subjects. On the other hand, the Burgundian kingdom was a well-established federate kingdom in a relatively fertile and rich region, so it might well be that the Burgundians had adopted the use of this Roman money and readily accepted the imposition of money compositions. In order to get some conception of the value of these coins to the Burgundians, we might note some of the wergelds and compositions.

Wergelds:

The Unfree (wergeld would be paid to master):

　　An ordinary slave—30 solidi

　　A slave, Roman or barbarian, ploughman or swineherd—30 solidi

　　A slave carpenter—40 solidi

　　A slave blacksmith—50 solidi

　　A slave silversmith—100 solidi

　　A slave goldsmith—200 solidi

　　A trained house servant or messenger (barbarian)—60 solidi

in suits involving less than ten solidi, let smaller payments be sought.

8. Since a similar condition has been forbidden among Romans in cases of the crime of venality, we command that Romans be judged by the Roman laws just as has been established by our predecessors; let them know that they must follow the form and statement of the written law when they render decisions so that no one may be excused on grounds of ignorance.

9. In the case of unjust decisions rendered before this time, let the conditions of the earlier law be followed. But we add this also, that if perchance a judge has been accused of corruption and has been convicted without sufficient reason, let the accuser be compelled to receive a punishment similar to that which we ordered the corrupted judge to receive.

10. If indeed anything is not covered by the statement of our laws, we order those judging to refer such matters to us.

11. Indeed if any judge, barbarian as well as Roman, shall not render decisions according to those provisions which the laws contain because he has been prevented by ignorance or negligence, and he has been diverted from justice for this reason, let him know that he must pay thirty solidi and that the case must be judged again on behalf of the aggrieved parties.

12. We apply this principle: if judges have entertained an appeal for the third time and have not rendered judgment, and if he who has brought suit believes that an appeal to us should be sought, and if he has proved his judges to have been present three times and not to have heard the case, let the judge suffer a fine of twelve

---

A royal agent (steward)—150 solidi
A private person's agent (steward)—100 solidi

The Freemen:
    Lower class (*minores personae*)—150 solidi
    Middle class (*mediocres*)—200 solidi
    Nobility (*optimates*)—300 solidi

Compositions in case of theft:

A bondservant—25 solidi	A sheep—1 solidus
A "best" horse—10 solidi	A beehive—1 solidus
An ordinary horse—5 solidi	A goat—1 tremissis
A mare—3 solidi	A dog—5 solidi
An ox—2 solidi	A falcon—6 solidi
A cow—1 solidus	A ship—12 solidi
A pig—1 solidus	A boat—2 solidi

solidi. But if anyone shall presume to come to us concerning any sort of case without consulting the judges—that is, not having appealed the case for a third time as we have ordered—let him pay the fine which we ordered a negligent judge to pay so that business may not be delayed through avoidance of the appointed judges.

13. Let no Roman or Burgundian count, in the absence of the other judge, presume to decide any case however often they may desire it, so that consulting frequently they may not be in doubt concerning the provisions of the laws.[5]

14. Finally it is pleasing that our constitutions be confirmed with the signatures of the counts added below, so that this statement of the law which has been written as the result of our effort and with the common consent of all may, observed throughout posterity, maintain the validity of a lasting agreement.

Here follow the names of those who have signed the laws and ensuing constitutions and those things which are set forth in the previous pages and which are to be observed in time to come under the guidance of God.

(At this point are appended the seals of the following counts)

Abcar	Wallaer
Aunemund	Siggo
Unnan	Fredemund
Hildeulf	Avenahar
Hildegern	Vulfia
Usgild	Sigisvuld
Walest	Sunia
Aumemund	Gundeful
Andar	Gundemund
Amgath	Effo
Auderic	Widemer
Aumemund	Wadahamer
Aveliemer	Silvan
Conigasd	Fastila
Viliemer	Coma
Coniaric	

[5] Evidently it was the custom for the justices to sit in pairs, perhaps one Burgundian count and one Roman count making up the court. Cf. G. A. Davoud-Oghlou, *Histoire de la Législation des Anciens Germains*, I, 435 (P, 2, 3).

I

OF THE PRIVILEGE OF BESTOWING GIFTS PERMITTED TO FATHERS, AND CONCERNING ROYAL GIFTS AND GRATUITIES.

1. Because nothing concerning the privilege of bestowing gifts which is permitted to fathers, or concerning the gifts (and gratuities) of rulers, has been provided in the laws, we have decreed in the present statute, with the common consent and will of all, that it be permitted to a father to give to anyone from the common property or from the produce of his labor before he makes a division, except that land acquired by allotment (title of lot, *sors*),[1] concerning which the arrangement of previous laws will still stand.[2]

2. If a father has divided (his property) with his sons and offered them their portions, and afterward had one or more sons by another wife, those sons who are by the second wife shall succeed to that portion which the father has acquired (subsequent to the first division)[3]: and when the father makes a division of his property, these children (of the second wife) can require nothing more from the other children.

3. Also it is pleasing that this rule be added to the law, that if any one of our people is known to have received anything in the way of gift from our predecessors, we decree in the present statute that he pass on to his sons that which was given to him out of our largesse.[4]

4. Moreover we decree that if anyone has received anything either from our gift, or shall receive otherwise, God granting, let the text of our gift show it. Further, let it be said that such gifts shall pass to their posterity provided they serve with such devotion and faith

---

[1] The land designated *terra sortis* was that land which a barbarian "guest" was assigned from the property of his Roman "host," according to the system of hospitality followed in dividing the land between the Burgundians and Romans. Among the Burgundians and Romans the practice seems to have been that the Burgundian received two-thirds of the land and one-third of the slaves of his Roman host. Cf. LIV, 1.

[2] See XIV, XLII, LI, LIII, LXII, LXXV, and LXXVIII.

[3] I.e., apparently that property acquired subsequent to the division among the sons of the first wife.

[4] Those who had received land from the king's grant were not allowed to share the property of a Roman host. Cf. LIV, 1.

that these gifts of our predecessors may be increased and preserved.[5]

II

OF MURDERS.[1]

1. If anyone presumes with boldness or rashness bent on injury to kill a native freeman of our people of any nation [2] or a servant of the king, in any case a man of barbarian tribe, let him make restitution for the committed crime not otherwise than by the shedding of his own blood.

2. We decree that this rule be added to the law by a reasonable provision, that if violence shall have been done by anyone to any person, so that he is injured by blows of lashes or by wounds, and if he pursues his persecutor and overcome by grief and indignation kills him, proof of the deed shall be afforded by the act itself or by suitable witnesses who can be believed. Then the guilty party shall be compelled to pay to the relatives of the person killed half his wergeld according to the status of the person: that is, if he shall have killed a noble of the highest class (*optimas nobilis*), we decree that the payment be set at one hundred fifty solidi, i.e., half his wergeld; if a person of middle class (*mediocris*), one hundred solidi; if a person of the lowest class (*minor persona*), seventy-five solidi.

3. If a slave unknown to his master presumes to kill a native freeman, let the slave be handed over to death, and let the master not be made liable for damages.

4. If the master knows of the deed, let both be handed over to death.

5. If the slave himself flees (*defuerit*) after the deed, let his master be compelled to pay thirty solidi to the relatives of the man killed for the value (wergeld) of the slave.

6. Similarly in the case of royal slaves, in accordance with the

---

[5] Davoud-Oghlou regards this law as an indication of incipient feudalism, for it seems to say that those who held land of the king owed some service in return. Cf. Davoud-Oghlou, *op. cit.*, I, 428 (0, 13), 446 (S, 5).

---

[1] These killings (*homicidia*) are apparently murders, not unpremeditated homicides.

[2] Nation, i.e., barbarian nation or tribe.

status of such persons, let the same condition about murderers be observed.

7. In such cases let all know this must be observed carefully, that the relatives of the man killed must recognize that no one can be pursued except the killer; because just as we have ordered the criminals to be destroyed, so we will suffer the innocent to sustain no injury.

III

OF THE EMANCIPATION OF OUR SLAVES.

If it shall be established that any were the freedmen or freedwomen of our ancestors of royal memory, that is, Gibica, Godomar, Gislaharius, Gundaharius, also of our father and our uncle, let them remain in that same state of freedom; whoever among them has been in a servitude of lower status under our ancestors, let them remain under our dominion (*dominium*).

IV

OF SOLICITATIONS AND THEFTS.

1. If anyone solicits another's bondservant, or anyone, either native Burgundian or Roman, presumes to take in theft a horse, mare, ox, or cow, let him be killed: and let him who lost the bondservants and animals mentioned above, if he is not able to find them in the possession of the solicitor or thief, receive compensation in fee simple: that is, if he is not able to find that bondservant, for the bondservant, twenty-five solidi; for the best horse, ten solidi; for an ordinary one, five solidi; for the mare, three solidi; for the ox, two solidi; for the cow, one solidus.

2. If indeed a slave commits the theft, let him be handed over to death: and let the master of the slave requite by a single payment (i.e., in fee simple) and without claim to further damages him who lost those things which were taken away by theft, including the above-mentioned animals which cannot be found, in accordance with the tariff of established prices.

3. And if any native freeman, either Burgundian or Roman, takes in theft a pig, a sheep, a beehive, or a she-goat, let him pay threefold according as their value is established, and in addition, let him pay a fine of twelve solidi. Let the composition be for the pig, one solidus; for the sheep, one solidus; for the beehive, one solidus; for the goat, a tremissis. Indeed, let their value be paid threefold.

4. If a slave of a Burgundian or of a Roman admits the theft of the afore-mentioned animals (livestock), let the slave be handed over for punishment that he may receive three hundred blows of a stick. Moreover, let the master pay in simple for the crime; and a fine is not required from the master.

5. If a native freeman steals the little bell (*tintinnum*)[1] attached to a horse, let him return another horse like it (i.e., a horse like the one to which the bell was attached); and let a like provision be observed concerning a lead ox. If a slave take it, let him be beaten.

6. Moreover, if a native freeman steals the hobble (*pedica*)[2] of a hobbled horse, let him know that a horse of like value must be returned. If a slave commits such an act, let him receive a hundred blows of a stick for each offense.

7. If a native freeman presumes to ride a horse without the owner's permission, let him know that two solidi must be given to him to whom the horse belongs if the horse has been taken for a journey of one day only; but if indeed for more than that, let him be held according to that law which we have ordered to be observed concerning horses used for journeys.[3] If a slave does this, let him be beaten.

---

[1] Cf. DuCange, *op. cit.*, VI, 592.

[2] Cf. *ibid.*, V, 173. It is suggested by Davoud-Oghlou that the heavy payment imposed for the theft of a little bell or a hobble—the value of the animal to which it was attached—results from the fact that the animal could easily become lost without the *tintinnum* or *pedica*. Cf. Davoud-Oghlou, *op. cit.*, I, 415 (L, 11).

[3] The word used here is *inventicius* which is very obscure. The root seems to be the same as that of *adventicius*, from which is derived the Castilian word *adventicio*, meaning something strange or unusual; the Portuguese word *adventicio* (*adventiciamente*), meaning adventitious, foreign, strange, extraordinary; and the Italian word *adventiccio*, which seems to mean a stranger, one who has come from abroad. Cf. DuCange, *op. cit.*, I, 97. Substituting the prefix *in* for *ad*, we get a word meaning something or someone coming from within and, when applied to a horse, might refer to a horse used for journeys within the realm or district under consideration. An alternative possibility

8. Let him who presumes to do work with the ox of another without the owner's knowledge or permission be compelled to hand over two oxen to the owner.

V

OF THOSE WHO STRIKE OTHERS WITH LASH OR ROD, WITH A KICK, OR WITH A BLOW OF THE FIST.

1. If anyone strikes a native freeman with such presumption, let him pay a single solidus for each blow, and let him render a fine of six solidi to the king's treasury.

2. Whoever strikes another's freedman, let him pay a single semissis for each blow; moreover, let the fine be set at four solidi.

3. Whoever strikes another's slave, let him pay a single tremissis for each blow; moreover, let the fine be set at three solidi.

4. If anyone seizes a native freeman violently by the hair, if with one hand, let him pay two solidi; if with both hands, four solidi; moreover, let the fine be set at six solidi.

5. If anyone seizes a freedman or another's slave violently by the hair, either with one hand or with both, it is pleasing that determination of punishment be made as in the case of blows, whether against a freeman, a freedman, or a slave, and so also assessment of both composition and fine is required in cases of this kind.

6. If a slave strikes a native freeman with a blow of his fist, let him receive a hundred blows.

7. If indeed a master of a slave engages in a fight (is hard pressed in a struggle) with another and the slave, while wishing to help his master, strikes his master's opponent, let the master pay one solidus for the blow struck by the slave.

---

deriving the word from *vendo* rather than *venio* might give the meaning of "riding horse," "livery horse," or a horse "for hire" as related to *venditio* (sale, for sale) or *ventitio* (customs, tax, payment) for which see *ibid.*, VI, 768. Davoud-Oghlou, *op. cit.*, I, 415 (L, 12) suggests only that the man who keeps a horse more than one day shall be considered a thief.

VI

OF FUGITIVES.

1. If anyone seizes a fugitive within the provinces belonging to us, let him receive a solidus for the fugitive; and if the fugitive takes a horse with him, let him (the man who seizes the fugitive) receive a semissis for a pack horse, a tremissis for a mare, and let him return the fugitive with all these things. And if it is without the realm, let him who seizes a fugitive receive two solidi for the fugitive, and for the horse one solidus, for the mare a semissis.

2. Let him who has followed a fugitive, and by chance kills him while resisting, be free from all blame (prosecution); or if he who follows is struck by the fugitive, let no blame attach to the master of the fugitive.

3. If a fugitive is captured by anyone, either Burgundian or Roman, and he escapes his custody by chance, let him from whom he fled swear that he had escaped without his collusion or knowledge, and after an oath has been given as stated above, let him suffer no blame.

4. Whoever unintentionally provides a native freeman or slave who is a fugitive with false hair (*capillum fecerit*),[1] let him forfeit five solidi; if he provides him with such hair intentionally, let him be compelled to pay the wergeld of the fleeing man.

5. Whoever intentionally aids a fugitive to cross a river, let him suffer the punishment of an accomplice (solicitor).

6. If a fugitive shall escape, let him (from whose custody he fled) take oath that the escape was made neither by his own collusion, as stated above, nor by the collusion of his slaves, and that he escaped his bonds neither with his nor with their knowledge.

---

[1] There is some difficulty with the phrase *capillum fecerit*, but it probably means "to provide with false hair," i.e., with a wig. Since loss of the hair was particularly degrading to a barbarian, it might well be that a slave might have his head shaved and that he would need a wig to conceal the fact that he was a fugitive slave. But the law mentions *freeman* or slave. Here we can only guess that the freeman had been apprehended for some crime and had his head shaved, and then escaped; or simply that he wanted a wig to conceal or disguise his identity. For other possibilities, cf. Davoud-Oghlou, *op. cit.*, I, 417, n. 1.

7. If indeed he will not give such an oath, let him pay fifteen solidi for the fugitive.

8. But if it happens that he (the fugitive) escaped with his collusion, he who allowed him to escape shall be compelled to pay thirty solidi. If indeed he who is seized takes with him something belonging to his master or to another and exhibits it in the house of the man from whose custody he escaped (with his consent), let that man restore it singlefold.

9. If a native freeman intentionally gives bread to a fugitive of a Burgundian or of a Roman, let him bring him back. If unintentionally he gives him bread, or helps him across a river, or shows him the road, let him suffer no loss after an oath has been given.

10. If a native freeman, knowing him to be a fugitive, gives letters [2] to the fugitive to aid his escape, let him be condemned to the loss of a hand; if a slave does this, let him be condemned to the loss of a hand after receiving three hundred blows.

VII

OF SLAVES (*Servi*) AND SERFS (*Originarii*) WHO ARE ACCUSED OF CRIMES.[1]

This procedure will be observed among Burgundians and Romans: if a crime is charged by anyone which cannot be proved at the present, we order that it be observed that whether it be the slave (*servus*) of Burgundian or Roman who is accused of the crime, let his master not be compelled to take oath either for slave (*servus*) or serf (*originarius*); but when a crime has been charged,

---

[2] Perhaps letters of direction or just possibly forged documents of manumission.

---

[1] At this period there is no clear distinction between the *servi* and *mancipia* in the unfree status and between the *coloni* and *originarii* in the semifree status. That this is true is quite clear in this law where *servi* and *mancipia* seem to be used interchangeably, while the same thing is true of *coloni* and *originarii*. Perhaps it is a mistake, however, to translate *colonus* and *originarius* as "serf," for they are not yet serfs in a strictly medieval sense; they are closer to the unfree in status and might even be sold away from the land with which they were associated. For *servus*, cf. DuCange, *op. cit.*, VI, 221; for *mancipium, ibid.*, IV, 218; for *colonus, ibid.*, II, 441; and for *originarius, ibid.*, IV, 734. Cf. LXXVII.

either let the value of the slave (*servus*) or serf (*colonus*) be established according to his condition, which (value) the master to whom the slave (*servus*) or serf (*colonus*) belongs shall receive from the accuser in person, or let him (the master) receive a slave (*mancipium*) of like value. When this has been done thus, let him who has been charged with the crime be handed over to a judge for torture so that if he shall have admitted by confession that which is charged, let the man (who brought the charge) receive back the wergeld which he had given (to the master of the slave). Then let the slave (*servus*) be killed for the confessed crimes so that the penalty which has been established above may be observed. But if, however, the slave (*servus*) or serf (*colonus*) shall not have confessed under torture, let him who made the charge make restitution to his master: let the master obtain either a substitute slave (*servus*), whom he receives on account of the punishment of an innocent slave (*servus*), or let him keep the wergeld (which the man who brought the charge was obliged to give the master of the slave against whom the charge was brought).

VIII

OF THE COMMISSION OF CRIMES WHICH ARE CHARGED AGAINST NATIVE FREEMEN.[1]

1. If a native freeman, either barbarian or Roman, is accused of a crime through suspicion, let him render oath, and let him swear with his wife and sons and twelve relatives: if indeed he does not have wife and sons and he has mother or father, let him complete the designated number with father and mother. But if he has neither father nor mother, let him complete the oath with twelve relatives.

2. But if he who must take oath wishes to take it with raised hand (*de manu*), and if those who are ordered to hear the oath—those three whom we always command to be delegated by the judges for hearing an oath—before they enter the church declare they do not wish to receive the oath, then he who was about to take oath is not permitted to do so after this statement, but they (the

[1] Cf. XLV.

judges) are hereby directed by us to commit the matter to the judgment of God (i.e., to ordeal).

3. If however, having received permission, he has taken the oath, and if he has been convicted after the oath, let him know that he must make restitution by a ninefold payment (*in novigildo*) to those in whose presence the judge ordered him to give his oath.

4. But if they (those appointed to hear the oath) fail to come to the place on the appointed day, and if they shall not have been detained by any illness or public duty, let them pay a fine of six solidi. But if they were detained by any illness or duty, let them make this known to the judge or send other persons in their place whom they can trust to receive the oath for them.

5. If moreover he who is about to take the oath does not come to the place, let the other party wait until the sixth hour of the day; but if he has not come by the sixth hour, let the case be dismissed without delay.

6. But if the other (the accusing party) does not come, let him who was about to take the oath depart without loss.

IX

OF ACTS OF VIOLENCE.

If any Burgundian or Roman shall take away anything, even a young animal, we order him who took it away to pay the price which has been set by us ninefold.

X

LET BURGUNDIANS AND ROMANS BE HELD UNDER THE SAME CONDITION IN THE MATTER OF KILLING SLAVES.

1. If anyone kills a slave, barbarian by birth, a trained (select) house servant or messenger, let him compound sixty solidi; moreover, let the amount of the fine be twelve solidi. If anyone kills another's slave, Roman or barbarian, either ploughman or swineherd, let him pay thirty solidi.

2. Whoever kills a skilled goldsmith, let him pay two hundred solidi.

3. Whoever kills a silversmith, let him pay one hundred solidi.
4. Whoever kills a blacksmith, let him pay fifty solidi.
5. Whoever kills a carpenter, let him pay forty solidi.

XI

OF INFLICTED WOUNDS.

1. Whoever cuts off with a blow the arm of a man, either a freeman or slave, let him compound half his wergeld; if he does not cut the arm off, let him be judged according to the nature of the wound.
2. If anyone inflicts a wound on another's face, we order him to pay three times the price in fee simple established for wounds on a part which is protected by clothing.

XII

OF THE STEALING OF GIRLS.

1. If anyone shall steal a girl, let him be compelled to pay the price set for such a girl ninefold, and let him pay a fine to the amount of twelve solidi.
2. If a girl who has been seized returns uncorrupted to her parents, let the abductor compound six times the wergeld of the girl; moreover, let the fine be set at twelve solidi.
3. But if the abductor does not have the means to make the above-mentioned payment, let him be given over to the parents of the girl that they may have the power of doing to him whatever they choose.
4. If indeed, the girl seeks the man of her own will and comes to his house, and he has intercourse with her, let him pay her marriage price threefold; if moreover, she returns uncorrupted to her home, let her return with all blame removed from him.
5. If indeed a Roman girl, without the consent or knowledge of her parents, unites in marriage with a Burgundian, let her know she will have none of the property of her parents.

XIII

OF CLEARINGS (*Exarti*).

If anyone, Burgundian as well as Roman, makes a clearing in the common forest, let him give another such tract of forest to his host (or guest as the case may be), and let him possess the clearing which he made without any disturbance [1] by his host (or guest).

XIV

OF SUCCESSION.

1. Among Burgundians we wish it to be observed that if anyone does not leave a son, let a daughter succeed to the inheritance of the father and mother in place of the son.

2. If by chance the dead leave neither son nor daughter, let the inheritance go to the sisters or nearest relatives.

3. It is pleasing that it be contained in the present law that if a woman having a husband dies without children, the husband of the dead wife may not demand back the marriage price (*pretium*) which had been given for her.

4. Likewise, let neither the woman nor the relatives of the woman seek back that which a woman pays when she comes to her husband if the husband dies without children.

5. Concerning those women who are vowed to God and remain in chastity, we order that if they have two brothers they receive a third portion of the inheritance of the father, that is, of that land which the father, possessing by the right of *sors* (allotment), left at the time of his death. Likewise, if she has four or five brothers, let her receive the portion due to her.

6. If moreover she has but one brother, let not a half, but a third part go to her on the condition that, after the death of her who

---

[1] Here for the word *commotione* Beyerle substitutes *communione,* a reading given by the larger number of manuscripts (A 3, B 2, 3, 11; *communionem* A 4, B 1, 8; *commune* B 5). This would change the law to read: "If anyone, Burgundian as well as Roman, makes a clearing in the common forest, let him give another such tract of forest to his host (or guest as the case may be) and let him possess the clearing which he made without any community of possession shared with his host (or guest)." Cf. Franz Beyerle, *Gesetze der Burgunden, Germanenrechte,* Band 10, 28; and DeSalis, *op. cit.,* p. 52.

is a woman and a nun, whatever she possesses in usufruct from her father's property shall go to the nearest relatives, and she will have no power of transferring anything therefrom, unless perhaps from her mother's goods, that is, from her clothing or things of the cell (*rescellulae*),[1] or what she has acquired by her own labor.

7. We decree that this should be observed only by those whose fathers have not given them portions; but if they shall have received from their father a place where they can live, let them have full freedom of disposing of it at their will.

XV

OF STARTING A FIGHT.

1. If any freeborn Burgundian enters another's house to fight, let him pay six solidi to him to whom the house belongs; and let the fine be twelve solidi. Furthermore we wish this to be observed equally among Burgundians and Romans.

2. Indeed if a slave enters another's house by force or violence, let him receive a hundred blows for punishment, and let the master of the slave suffer no loss on that account.

XVI

OF HUNTING FOR ANIMALS.

1. If anyone has followed the tracks of an animal, and following those tracks comes to another's house, and if he to whose house he comes prohibits his entering the house to seek back his property, let him who drives him away from his house when he is making inquiry about that which he seeks back be held for punishment as a thief, with the further provision that it is not permitted a woman to deny questioning (to refuse to reply to an inquiry).

2. But if perhaps a slave or a maidservant prohibits this when his or her master is absent, let him who prohibits it be held by law liable to punishment as a thief.

[1] *Rescellulae* seems to be a compound of *res* and *cellulae*. *Res* is the classical Latin "things" while *cellula* is vulgar Latin for "nun's room" or "apartment." So *rescellulae* may mean "things" or "trappings of the cell."

3. If there is a way-pointer (tracker, *veius*)[1] present and he has received his payment (*vegiatura*) and he to whom he points the way is not able to find them (the animals), let the way-pointer (tracker, *veius*) pay for the theft in fee simple because he lies that he has pointed the way to them.

XVII

Of Other Cases and the Removal of Liability for Punishment.

1. All cases which involve Burgundians and which were not completed before the Battle of Chalons [1] are declared dismissed.
2. If anyone shall identify his slave or maidservant, let him receive him back.[2]
3. For a freeman killed previously twenty solidi may be imposed and let all further prosecution cease.
4. And also we wish it to be particularly observed, that if any Burgundian has been twice admonished for any cause by him who brings a case against him that he should come to court and provide a guarantor (oathtaker) and, if he does not provide a guarantor (oathtaker) or come to court, and the summoner is able

---

[1] Cf. DuCange, *op. cit.*, VI, 753–54. The word *vegius* seems to refer to some type of soothsayer, prophet, or diviner (*harioli, vates, divini*) whom the Saxons call *vigileri* and the Germans *viclers*, whence *viglias* means soothsayers, for these consult the auspices to determine whether slaves and animals have been taken away by theft so that they might point out where they are. The payment for providing this information is called *vegiaturum*. Others deduce a meaning from the Saxon word *veg* or *vaeg*, which means a road, thus they are road-pointers (*vegii*) who point out the tracks of animals. Cf. XCV.

---

[1] The Battle of Chalons or of Mauriac (the *Lex Gundobada* refers to it as *pugna Mauriacensis*) is the battle which took place in 451 in which a federate army of Romans and barbarians under Aetius faced an invasion of the Huns who, under their leader, Attila, were threatening to subjugate all of Gaul. To face this threat, Aetius got together an army consisting of imperial troops and Franks, Burgundians, Bretons, and Visigoths. The Huns were turned back at Chalons, but Theodoric, king of the Visigoths and the most influential of the barbarian leaders at this time, was killed. That the date 451 seemed an important one to the barbarians is attested by the fact that the year 451 is a delimiting date in the *Lex Gundobada* and in the Visigothic Code of Euric. Cf. *Frag. Visig.* (*Antiqua*, ed. Bluhme, p. 4).

[2] Davoud-Oghlou suggests that a master may seek back such an identified slave even when the loss of the slave dated prior to the Battle of Chalons. Cf. Davoud-Oghlou, *op. cit.*, I, 420 (L, 48).

to prove this fact with two or three native freeborn witnesses, let him (the man who refused to come to court) pay a fine of six solidi and nonetheless be compelled to come to judgment.

5. With the further condition that a Roman freeman who has a case with a barbarian (serf) should admonish either his master or his overseer (*actor*), and if the overseer shall not come after he has been admonished repeatedly (twice?) to reply to the charge in behalf of the serf (*originarius*) committed to him, let the overseer receive a hundred blows.

XVIII

OF THOSE THINGS WHICH HAPPEN BY CHANCE.

1. If any animal by chance, or if any dog by bite, causes death to a man, we order that among Burgundians the ancient rule of blame [1] be removed henceforth: because what happens by chance ought not to conduce to the loss or discomfiture of man. So that if among animals, a horse kills a horse unexpectedly, or an ox gores an ox, or a dog gnaws a dog, so that it is crippled, let the owner hand over the animal or dog through which the loss is seen to have been committed to him who suffers the loss. [2]

2. In truth, if a lance or any kind of weapon shall have been thrown upon the ground or set there without intent to do harm (*simpliciter*), and if by accident a man or animal impales himself thereupon, we order that he to whom the weapon belongs shall pay nothing unless by chance he held the weapon in his own hands in such a manner that it could cause harm to a man.

[1] By the phrase "the ancient rule of blame" perhaps this statute is referring to the earlier customary law of the Burgundians that was in effect among the people of that tribe before they entered the Roman Empire and came into contact with the written Roman law. Perhaps this is a reference to the early Germanic *faida* or law of revenge, for our law here seems to imply that under the "ancient rule of blame" a man was held personally accountable for the actions of his animals. Cf. *ibid.*, I (C, 2).

[2] DeSalis, *op. cit.*, p. 56, n. 3, suggests that it is probable that the legislator wished to follow the Roman law in this instance since he states specifically that the ancient Burgundian law has been abolished or replaced.

XIX

OF THE REMOVAL OF PLEDGES AND GUARANTORS (OATHTAKERS).

1. If anyone removes pledges of any sort whatsoever before the hearing, let him lose his case, and let him pay a fine of twelve solidi.

2. If anyone takes another's horse as if identified for his own, and is not able to prove it his, let him be sentenced to the loss of another (additional) horse of like worth.

3. If anyone receives pledges (*pigneraverit*) (from a third party) in behalf of him with whom he thinks he has a case and he does not have a case with that person, if he has taken horses or oxen or seized a bondservant, let him pay two solidi for each bondservant and animal (and return the pledges).[1]

4. If he has taken a native freeborn person as a pledge, let him pay four solidi for this presumption.

5. If anyone is a guarantor (oathtaker) for his relative, or friend, or for anyone for any debt whatsoever, and if he (the debtor) who has departed while under oath (pledge) has been warned three times in the presence of witnesses, and if he (the debtor), still under pledge after this warning, has been convicted of removing the pledges of his guarantor (oathtaker) by force, so that it was necessary that the guarantor (oathtaker) be bound and forced to pay the debt from his own property, then let whatever it has been established that the guarantor (oathtaker) paid in this case be rendered threefold by him in whose behalf he took the oath (or, in whose behalf he gave pledges).

6. The manner of giving pledges shall be this: let the guarantor (oathtaker) raise a third part more than the sum of the debt (i.e., the total debt) and let him make declaration to the debtor in the presence of witnesses. But if when the debt has been paid, he (the guarantor) shall not take back his pledges within three months thereafter, he shall no longer have the right (*pontificium*) [2] of seeking them back.

---

[1] The law does not specifically state "and return the pledges," but it is obviously implied. Cf. Davoud-Oghlou, *op. cit.*, I, 450 (T, 4).

[2] For this unusual meaning of the word *pontificium* as *potestas* or *jus*, cf. DuCange, *op. cit.*, V, 347. See also Title XL, 1.

7. If he who offers a guarantor (oathtaker) does not have the wherewith to pay, let the guarantor (oathtaker) hand the debtor over to the creditor to clear himself, and let nothing else be required from the guarantor (oathtaker).

8. But if he has failed to pay what it has been established that he owes (*quod placitum est*), and it shall be necessary that the guarantor (oathtaker) be bound and compelled to pay the debt from his own property, let satisfaction be received by the guarantor who offered the oath (or pledges) threefold whatever it is established he has paid in this case.

9. If any guarantor (oathtaker) hands over a debtor's property to him to whom the guarantor (oathtaker) has given pledges, let him bring it up to the creditor's house in his own defense (to satisfy his obligation); if he does not do it, let him not be wholly released from his obligation.

10. If a guarantor (oathtaker) does not wish to render satisfaction in a debtor's behalf, under circumstances where it shall be necessary that the guarantor (oathtaker) pledge his own property, and if the guarantor (oathtaker) wishes to resist, let him make satisfaction (to the creditor) from his own property in such amount as may be demanded from him on account of his oath (i.e., as due on his oath).

11. If a debtor places a guarantor (oathtaker) under pledge and he (the debtor) in whose behalf the guarantor (oathtaker) has given pledges shall believe that the pledges of his guarantor (oathtaker) or his own pledges, if the guarantor (oathtaker) has given them, may be taken away or destroyed, let him pay ninefold the amount he is convicted of taking away and let him pay a fine in the sum of twelve solidi.

XX

Of Thefts Committed by Fugitives.

1. If any slave has fled, and while in flight steals any ornaments, clothes, or anything belonging to anyone and takes them with him, let none of these things be sought back from the master of the slave; provided only that if the master is able to recall him

from his flight and the slave is convicted of having stolen anything, let him (the master) make restitution in fee simple.

2. If a slave has committed the theft while under the dominion (*in obsequio*) of his master, and if he flees after committing the theft, let his master prove by oaths that he should not be held liable to punishment either for the theft or for the flight of the slave because of his own knowledge about the matter. But when he has given oath, nothing may then be sought from the master of the slave.

3. Indeed, those who seize fugitives must send them back to their masters; and besides that solidus which is due for a fugitive within the realm, he shall receive a solidus for a journey of one hundred miles [1] on which he has sent some messenger or brought news of the matter himself.

4. But if he does not deliver him and the fugitive escapes, and if he has not delivered him within thirty days, let him absolve himself either by oaths as stated above, or let him pay fifteen solidi for the fugitive.

XXI

OF CONTRACTS ENTERED INTO BY SLAVES.

1. If anyone, Burgundian as well as Roman, lends money to a serf or slave without consulting his master, let him lose the money.

2. Indeed whoever has permitted a slave to exercise his assigned occupation in public as gold, silver, iron, or bronze smith, tailor or shoemaker, and perchance the slave destroys what he has received from anyone to work upon, let his master render satisfaction for the same, or if he chooses, let him give up the servant to the man who has suffered loss.

---

[1] The Latin here is not clear as to whether it means that the man will receive a solidus for each hundred miles which he travels, or whether he will receive a solidus for a journey of a hundred miles or more. The first alternative seems the more probable.

XXII

Of the Abolition of the Advocacy (*Patrocinium*) [1] of Barbarians in Lawsuits Involving Romans.

Whatever Roman hands over a case which he has with another Roman to be transacted by a Burgundian as advocate, let him lose the case, and let him who receives it pay a fine in the amount of twelve solidi.

XXIII

Of Injuries Which Are Caused by Animals.

1. If a man has enclosed or shut away an animal from his crops or from any place where it can do damage, and if the man to whom the animals belong drives them by force out of the courtyard of him who confined them as a voluntary act of presumption before the value of the damage done has been established, let him pay six solidi to him against whom he used force and let there be a fine of six solidi for the estimated loss. If a slave does this, let him receive a hundred blows; likewise concerning the estimated loss.

2. If any animal is impaled while being driven from a field, from a meadow, from a vineyard, or from a wheat field, let nothing be required from him who was driving it away.

3. But if a man undertakes to remove animals belonging to himself from a field or from any place while they are being guarded in an enclosure because of the damage they have done, let him pay a single tremissis for each animal, and let the amount of the fine be three solidi.

[1] The *patrocinium* or *advocatus* represents a wide variety of legal powers. The advocate was originally a person called or summoned (*advocatus*) by the injured party to assist at court, one who might exercise a moral influence on the judge because of his position or prestige. This advocacy was termed *patrocinium* in cases where the patron of an enfranchised serf acted as such an advocate. The custom of appearing and speaking in behalf of the client became established among the advocates and patrons who knew the laws better, owing to their social position and the fact that they had more talent in pleading cases before the courts. The personal relationship between patron and client involved in the *patrocinium* is generally regarded as one of the basic legal institutions which underlies the later feudal relation of lord and vassal. Cf. Davoud-Oghlou, *op. cit.*, I, 439, n. 2, and DuCange, *op. cit.*, V, 116.

4. If anyone's pigs have done damage in a vineyard, in the meadows, in the tilled fields, or in the acorn-bearing forests, and the master of the pigs has been warned twice that he must guard his pigs, and he does not wish to, let him to whom they did the damage have the power to kill the best from the herd of pigs and turn it to his own use.

5. But if there is no contest (i.e., the master has not been warned), and so the man damaged kills the pig, let him pay a solidus for the pig, with the further provision that that which the pigs have destroyed will be compounded.

XXIV

OF BURGUNDIAN WOMEN ENTERING A SECOND OR THIRD MARRIAGE.

1. If any Burgundian woman, as is the custom, enters a second or third marriage after the death of her husband, and she has children by each husband, let her possess the marriage gift (*donatio nuptialis*) in usufruct while she lives; after her death, let what his father gave her be given to each son, with the further provision that the mother has the power neither of giving, selling, or transferring any of the things which she received in the marriage gift.

2. If by chance the woman has no children, after her death let her relatives receive half of whatever has come to her by way of marriage gift, and let the relatives of the dead husband who was the donor receive half.

3. But if perchance children shall have been born and they shall have died after the death of their father, we command that the inheritance of the husband or children belong wholly to the mother. Moreover, after the death of the mother, we decree that what she holds in usufruct by inheritance from her children shall belong to the legal heirs of her children. Also we command that she protect the property of her children dying intestate.

4. If any son has given his mother something by will or by gift, let the mother have the power of doing whatever she wishes therewith; if she dies intestate, let the relatives of the woman claim the inheritance as their possession.

5. If any Burgundian has sons (children?) to whom he has given their portions, let him have the power of giving or selling that which he has reserved for himself to whomever he wishes.

XXV

Of Thefts and Acts of Violence.

1. If anyone enters a garden with violence, let him pay three solidi for such presumption to him to whom the garden belongs, and let the fine be six solidi.

2. If a slave does this, let him receive a hundred blows.

XXVI

Of Knocking Out Teeth.

1. If anyone by chance strikes out the teeth of a Burgundian of the highest class, or of a Roman noble, let him be compelled to pay fifteen solidi.

2. For middle-class freeborn people, either Burgundian or Roman, if a tooth is knocked out, let composition be made in the sum of ten solidi.

3. For persons of the lowest class, five solidi.[1]

---

[1] The divisions of Burgundian and Roman society in the realm of the Burgundians are not at all clear. In addition to the royal servants and officials mentioned in the preface, *Constitutiones Extravagantes* XXII, 14, and various laws throughout the *Lex Gundobada,* we have a more general division of all society into free and unfree with the *coloni* or *originarii* occupying a halfway position between those who were free and those who were not free. The present law, XXVI, deals with four classes of free men: the highest, middle, and lowest classes of men who were free from birth; and the freedmen or slaves who had been emancipated by their masters or who had earned their freedom in some way. The freedman is obviously quite low in the social scale when we observe these tariffs, but the children of freedmen were regarded as freemen, and even the freedman himself might gain that status following the death of his former master (cf. XL, 2). However, we have no indication as to how the distinctions among the freemen were determined. We may assume that the nobles, the *optimates,* constituted the highest class, but as for the two lower classes, there is no basis for the distinction stated anywhere in the *Lex Gundobada,* although from the tenor of the laws it seems that the middle class was more closely connected with the highest class than with the lowest class. The caste line between the free and unfree was sharply drawn, for the daughter of a freeman who united with a slave faced a penalty

4. If a slave voluntarily strikes out the tooth of a native freeman, let him be condemned to have a hand cut off; if the loss which has been set forth above has been committed by accident, let him pay the price for the tooth according to the status of the person.

5. If any native freeman strikes out the tooth of a freedman, let him pay him three solidi. If he strikes out the tooth of another's slave, let him pay two solidi to him to whom the slave belongs.

XXVII

OF BROKEN FENCES, CLOSED ROADS, ALSO THEFTS AND ACTS OF VIOLENCE.

1. If a native freeman breaks and opens another's fence when subject to no impedient (impairment) therefrom, only for the purpose of causing such damage, let him pay a single tremissis for each stake to him to whom the crop belongs; if a slave does this, let him receive a hundred blows, and let the fence which was broken be repaired.

2. We also command this to be observed concerning meadows and vineyards.

3. We wish all to recognize this: whoever blocks a public road (i.e., a main highway) or a country lane, let him know that he must pay a fine of twelve solidi, with the further consequence that the fence may be removed and the crops may be destroyed with impunity by travellers to the extent that they occupy space on the highway.

4. If a native freeman breaks another's fence and lets his horses or animals voluntarily into a field or meadow, he shall pay a single solidus for each animal for the damage to the crop or to the meadow.

5. If a slave does this, let him receive a hundred blows; and fur-

---

of death or perpetual servitude to the king (cf. XXXV, 2, 3), but intermarriage among the classes of freemen was evidently quite common. We have no indication as to what the status of the offspring of such a mixed marriage might be however. The chief distinction between the classes of freemen as far as the materials within the *Lex Gundobada* are concerned is the difference in the wergeld or value attached to the life of each man. Cf. II, 2.

thermore, let the damage which was done be compounded by the master of the slave.

6. If he to whom the horses belong is found by the owner of the meadow, and attempts to resist when he is held to an accounting, and if he shall then be slain or injured, let him to whom the field or meadow belongs suffer no loss (legal accountability) therefrom.

7. If anyone has entered another's vineyard secretly or violently by day so that he causes loss, let him pay three solidi for this presumption; if a slave does this, let him be killed.

8. If anyone at night has entered a vineyard bearing fruit and has been killed by the keeper of the vineyard within the vineyard, let nothing be required by the master or relatives of the man killed.

9. If a native freeman steals a ploughshare by theft, let him be compelled to give to the master two oxen with yoke and attachments (harness); if a slave does this, let him receive one hundred fifty blows of a stick.

XXVIII

Of the Privilege of Cutting Wood Granted in Common.

1. If any Burgundian or Roman does not have forest land, let him have the right to cut wood for his own use from fallen trees or trees without fruit in anyone's forest, and let him not be driven away by the owner of the forest.

2. If perchance anyone fells a fruit-bearing tree in another's forest without the owner's permission, let him pay the owner of the forest one solidus for each tree he has cut. We command this to be observed also with regard to pines and fir trees. But if a slave does this, let him be beaten and let his master suffer no loss or blame.

3. If anyone does not permit a man to take the wood necessary for his use from the fallen trees or those not bearing fruit, and if the man seeking wood offers pledges to him, let the pledges be returned threefold, and let a fine of six solidi be paid.

XXIX

Of Those Committing Assault and Breach of the Peace.

1. If anyone in an act of assault or robbery kills a merchant or anyone else, let him be killed; with the further condition that if those things which he took cannot be found, let them be compensated in fee simple from his property.

2. But if a man committing an assault shall have been killed by those whom he intended to rob, let no suit be brought for this reason against the killers by the master or relatives of the man killed.

3. We order all lawbreakers who plunder houses or treasure chests to be killed.

XXX

Of Women Violated.

1. Whatever native freeman does violence to a maidservant, and force can be proved, let him pay twelve solidi to him to whom the maidservant belongs.

2. If a slave does this, let him receive a hundred fifty blows.

XXXI

Of Planting Vineyards.

1. Among Burgundians and Romans, we order that the rule be observed that whoever plants a vineyard in a common field with no opposition shall restore a like field to him in whose holding he placed the vineyard.

2. If indeed after prohibition anyone presumes to plant a vineyard in another's field, let him lose his labor, and let him whose field it is receive the vineyard.

XXXII

Of Him Who Has Bound a Man Illegally or Without Cause.

1. If a native freeman binds an innocent native freeman, let him pay twelve solidi to him whom he bound, and let the amount of the fine be twelve solidi.

2. If he binds a freedman, let him pay six solidi to him whom he bound, and let the amount of the fine be six solidi.

3. If he binds a slave, let him pay him three solidi, and let the amount of the fine be three solidi.

4. If a slave does this, let him receive a hundred blows.

XXXIII

Of Injuries Which Are Suffered by Women.

1. If any native freewoman has her hair cut off and is humiliated without cause (when innocent) by any native freeman in her home or on the road, and this can be proved with witnesses, let the doer of the deed pay her twelve solidi, and let the amount of the fine be twelve solidi.

2. If this was done to a freedwoman, let him pay her six solidi.

3. If this was done to a maidservant, let him pay her three solidi, and let the amount of the fine be three solidi.

4. If this injury (shame, disgrace) is inflicted by a slave on a native freewoman, let him receive two hundred blows; if a freedwoman, let him receive a hundred blows; if a maidservant, let him receive seventy-five blows.

5. If indeed the woman whose injury we have ordered to be punished in this manner commits fornication voluntarily (i.e., if she yields), let nothing be sought for the injury suffered.

XXXIV

Of Divorces.

1. If any woman leaves (puts aside) her husband to whom she is legally married, let her be smothered in mire.

2. If anyone wishes to put away his wife without cause, let him give her another payment such as he gave for her marriage price, and let the amount of the fine be twelve solidi.

3. If by chance a man wishes to put away his wife, and is able to prove one of these three crimes against her, that is, adultery, witchcraft, or violation of graves, let him have full right to put her away: and let the judge pronounce the sentence of the law against her, just as should be done against criminals.

4. But if she admits none of these three crimes, let no man be per-

mitted to put away his wife for any other crime. But if he chooses, he may go away from the home, leaving all household property behind, and his wife with their children may possess the property of her husband.

XXXV

OF THE PUNISHMENT OF SLAVES WHO COMMIT A CRIMINAL ASSAULT ON FREEBORN WOMEN.

1. If any slave does violence to a native freewoman, and if she complains and is clearly able to prove this, let the slave be killed for the crime committed.
2. If indeed a native free girl unites voluntarily with a slave, we order both to be killed.
3. But if the relatives of the girl do not wish to punish their own relative, let the girl be deprived of her free status and delivered into servitude to the king.

XXXVI

OF INCESTUOUS ADULTERY.

If anyone has been taken in adultery with his relative or with his wife's sister, let him be compelled to pay her wergeld, according to her status, to him who is the nearest relative of the woman with whom he committed adultery; and let the amount of the fine be twelve solidi. Further, we order the adulteress to be placed in servitude to the king.

XXXVII

OF DRAWN SWORDS.

Anyone who draws out his sword or dagger for striking another, and does not strike him, let him pay a fine of twelve solidi. If he strikes him, let him likewise pay twelve solidi and be judged according to the inflicted wound.

XXXVIII

OF THE REFUSAL OF HOSPITALITY [1] TOWARD LEGATES OF FOREIGN TRIBES AND TRAVELLERS.

1. Whoever refuses his roof or hearth to a guest on arrival, let him be fined three solidi for the neglect.

2. If a member of the royal court be refused, let the amount of the fine be six solidi.

3. We wish it to be observed concerning the legates of foreign tribes, that wherever they take quarters, they have the right to expect one pig and one sheep; and let him who prohibits this from being done be compelled to pay a fine of six solidi.

4. And let him who made gifts to the legates be compensated by those who live within the boundaries of his village.

5. Moreover, if in the wintertime a legate asks for hay or barley, let this likewise be provided by those dwelling within the bounds of the village, Burgundian as well as Roman, without any refusal. We order this to be observed especially by people of higher rank.

6. If, however, he is a person who has been the beneficiary of our largesse and so can receive a legate, let him prepare a suitable lodging for a night for the legate at his own expense. But if he does not do this, let him know that a fine of twelve solidi must be paid.

---

[1] Hospitality here is used in the more general or common sense meaning that reception or kindness which is shown to a temporary guest. We have here something which resembles the later feudal duty of entertainment required of a vassal or a tenant. *Hospitalitas* was not only permitted to officials who were *in truste* of the king, but it was also extended to legates from abroad charged with missions to the king. All such persons enjoyed the full hospitality which the law imposed on the inhabitants of the districts through which they travelled. Cf. Davoud-Oghlou, *op. cit.,* I, 446. Indeed, the principle of *hospitalitas* seems to have been extended to all persons such as royal officers and personal legates who may be regarded as *in truste* of the king. These officials are apparently the Burgundian equivalents of the *antrustiones* among the Franks. Most of these officials were not only associated with the judicial system but also charged with administrative and police duties; furthermore, in time of war these trusted personal servants of the king acted as officers in command of the military forces, that is, the same officials acting in their military capacity in war may be described as *in hoste,* whereas in time of peace, they were declared to be *in truste* in the sense of persons in the intimate personal retinue of the king who enjoyed his trust and confidence.

7. If a man making a journey on private business comes to the house of a Burgundian and seeks hospitality and the latter directs him to the house of a Roman, and this can be proved, let the Burgundian pay three solidi to him to whose house he directed the traveller, and let the amount of the fine be three solidi.

8. If anyone seeks hospitality on the royal domain or at the dwelling of a serf (*colonus*) [2] and it is not granted, let the serf be beaten.

9. If moreover the guest destroys something insolently, let him restore it ninefold.

10. If there is a steward (*conductor*) in the village who is a native freeman, and he does not provide roof or hearth, let him pay a fine of three solidi. If he is a slave, let him be beaten.

11. We wish these things to be observed by the serfs and slaves of all Burgundians and Romans.

XXXIX

Of Receiving Strangers.

1. If anyone receives a stranger coming to him from any nation, let him present him to the judge for investigation so that he may confess under torture to whom he belongs.

2. But if anyone does not do this within seven days, and the matter is learned by the master of the slave, let him with whom the slave has been found be held to a triple payment of the slave's wergeld; those slaves are excepted who have been carried away into captivity and would return to their masters, relatives, and homes.

3. If however a stranger shall have been received or concealed by the agent or serf of anyone whomsoever without the master's knowledge, let the agent or serf receive three hundred blows; and

---

[2] Among the Merovingian Franks and probably also among the Burgundians, the *coloni* were lower in the social scale than the actually free men. The *coloni* were freeborn persons and were recognized as persons before the law, but they enjoyed only a limited freedom. They held land from which they could not be ejected, but which they might not leave. Even though they were left unharassed when they paid certain dues and performed certain duties, the fact that they were enrolled on the land deprived them of real freedom. Cf. Gregory of Tours, *The History of the Franks*, translation and introduction by O. M. Dalton, I, 391.

let the master support by oaths that he had no knowledge of the hiding place of the fugitive.

4. Thirdly, let the same condition be observed in the case of a bondservant as with captives, to the end that he to whom he came may not conceal him, but immediately take action to restore him to his master. But if he does not do this, let him restore the bondservant whom he had withheld to the detriment of his master with a double wergeld payment to the master.

5. But if a slave, unknown to his master, is convicted in the retention of a bondservant, let him receive two hundred blows.

XL

OF MANUMISSIONS.

1. If any Burgundian gives his liberty to a bondservant under his jurisdiction,[1] and if upon the occasion of a slight offense he thinks the servant ought to be recalled into servitude, let the manumitter know that he is denied this privilege by the present law; nor can the manumitter recall him to his original condition, unless by chance he has been convicted before a judge of having committed such acts to the loss and disgrace of his manumitter that he should deservedly lose the liberty conferred on him. Further, we order that the right (*pontificium*)[2] of this action be permitted to manumitters only in the case of their own freedmen.

2. Let the heirs of him by whom the bondservant has been freed know that in any lawsuit whatsoever the freedman of their father must be regarded as a freeman.

XLI

OF CROPS BURNED BY FIRE.

1. If anyone makes a fire in a clearing, and the fire, with no wind driving it, runs over the land and comes to another's fence or field, let whatever has been burned by it be replaced by him who started the fire.

---

[1] Beyerle, *op. cit.*, p. 61, suggests the translation, "If any Burgundian gives the freedom of his tribal law to a bondservant, and if . . ."

[2] Cf. DuCange, *op. cit.*, V, 347.

2. If indeed the force of the wind takes the fire to another's fence or field, let restitution for the damage which has been suffered not be sought from him who started the fire.

XLII

OF THE INHERITANCE OF THOSE WHO DIE WITHOUT CHILDREN.

1. Although we have ordered many things in former laws [1] concerning the inheritance of those who die without children, nevertheless after considering the matter thoroughly, we perceive it to be just that some of those things which were ordered before should be corrected. Therefore we decree in the present constitution that if a woman whose husband has died without children has not taken her vows a second time, let her possess securely a third of all the property of her husband to the day of her death; with the further provision that after her death, all will revert to the legitimate heirs of her husband.

2. Let that remain in effect which has been stated previously concerning the morning gift (*morgengeba, morginegiva*).[2] For if she wishes to marry within a year from the time of the death of her first husband, let her have full right to do so, but let her give up that third part of the property which she had been permitted to possess. However, if she wishes to take a husband after a year or two have passed, let her give up all as has been stated above which she

---

[1] Cf. XIV, 2.

[2] The word *pretium* is used to express the idea of a price or wergeld of the woman, but it also refers to the present made at the time of the marriage. Title XLII, 2, apparently defines the *morgengaba* as *pretium quod de nuptiis inferendum est*. This definition of *pretium* in the law seems to indicate that *pretium uxoris, pretium de nuptiis, morgengaba,* and *donatio nuptialis* designate the same general idea. However there are concrete distinctions: the *morgengaba* designates the present made the day after the wedding night; *pretium uxoris* is probably the price or wergeld of the woman; the *donatio nuptialis* is a present which is made at the occasion of the wedding by the parents of the husband to the woman, and by her parents to the husband; the *pretium de nuptiis* seems to be a general expression which includes the *wittimon, donatio,* and *morgengaba*. The *wittimon* is a payment made by the husband to the father of the bride and may correspond to the *pretium uxoris* or *nuptiale pretium*. For *pretium nuptiale*, see XII, 4; LII, 3; LXI; for *donatio nuptialis*, see XXIV, 1, 2; for *morgengaba*, see XLII, 2; for *wittimon*, see LXIX; LXXXVI, 2; and CI. Cf. Davoud-Oghlou, *op. cit.*, I, 430, n. 2.

received from her first husband, and let the heirs in whose portion the inheritance of her former husband belongs receive the price which must be paid for her (second) marriage.

Given in council at Ambérieux, September 3rd (501), Abienus *vir clarissimus* being consul.

XLIII

OF GIFTS.

1. Although our law prescribes many things concerning gifts set forth in earlier times, nevertheless because some things arise under the same heading concerning which the law is not clearly established, it is necessary that by the addition of the present law those things be defined which were formerly omitted. And therefore in this decree gifts and wills made among our people become valid provided five or seven witnesses to the gift or will append their marks and signatures so far as they are able.

2. But if a lesser number of witnesses is proved to have been present, let the gift which has been made, or the will which has been devised, be invalid.

3. Indeed in other instances, that is in lesser matters, we order three appropriate witnesses to be admitted.

4. And in other matters concerning wills and gifts, let the procedure established above be observed.

XLIV

OF THE ADULTERY OF GIRLS AND WIDOWS.

1. If the daughter of any native Burgundian before she is given in marriage unites herself secretly and disgracefully in adultery with either barbarian or Roman, and if afterward she brings a complaint, and the act is established as charged, let him who has been accused of her corruption, and as has been said, is convicted with certain proof, suffer no defamation of character (*calumnia*) upon payment of fifteen solidi. She indeed, defeated in her purpose by the vileness of her conduct, shall sustain the disgrace of lost chastity.

2. But if a widow who has not been sought, but rather overcome

by desire, unites with anyone, and she bursts forth in an accusing voice, let her not receive the stated number of solidi, and we order that she, demanding marriage thus, be not awarded to him to whom she joined herself in such a disgraceful manner, because it is just that she, defeated by her vile conduct, is worthy of neither matrimony nor reward.

XLV

OF THOSE WHO DENY THOSE THINGS CHARGED AGAINST THEM, AND OFFER OATHS.[1]

We know that many of our people are corrupted through inability to establish a case and because of instinct of greed, so that they do not hesitate frequently to offer oaths about uncertain matters and likewise to perjure themselves about known matters. To break up this criminal practice, we decree by the present law that as often as a case shall arise among our people and he who has been accused denies by offering oaths that that which is sought is owed by him, and that that has been done which is charged, it is fitting that an end be made to their litigation in this manner: if the party to whom oath has been offered does not wish to receive the oath, but shall say that the truthfulness of his adversary can be demonstrated only by resort to arms, and the second party (the one accused) shall not yield (the case charged), let the right of combat not be refused; with the further provision that one of the same witnesses who came to give oath shall fight, God being the judge. For it is just that if anyone shall say without delay that he knows the truth of the matter and shall offer to take oath, he should not hesitate to fight. But if the witness of him who offered oath was overcome in that combat, let all witnesses who promised that they would take oath be compelled to pay a fine of three hundred solidi without any grant of delay. But if he who refused to receive the oath (the accuser) shall have been killed, let the victorious party be repaid ninefold the sum (debt) involved taken from his property (i.e., from the property of the dead man) as damages, so that as a result, one may delight in truth rather than falsehood.

[1] Cf. VIII.

Given the 28th of May (502) at Lyons, Abienus *vir clarissimus* being consul.

XLVI

OF THOSE WHO SET TRAPS (DRAWN BOWS, *tensuras*) FOR KILLING WOLVES.[1]

1. It is fitting that those who create strife among our people or cause danger to men should be corrected reasonably by the prohibition of law. And therefore we order that from the present time anyone who sets a bow for the purpose of killing wolves should let those living round about know of it forthwith by giving warning on the same day. He should set up three bowstrings carefully so that they may serve as warning signs of the drawn bow, of which two (of the bowstrings) are placed higher up (above the ground). If these shall be touched by men coming upon them ignorantly, or by domestic animals, the bow will discharge the arrow harmlessly.

2. But if this has been done in the manner provided so that the set traps are known to those living round about, let him who set the bow sustain no criminal charges (*calumniae*) in the case of any native freeman who incautiously incurs death or injury from this cause; but he will take care to pay twenty-five solidi to the relatives of the man killed.

3. But if it is a slave who has been struck by the arrow, let him lie unavenged without any payment (i.e., uncompensated).

4. But if he who set the bow has not made it known to those living near by, and if the bowstrings were not placed with that care or in that manner which we ordered, and if any native freeman or slave has been killed, let him (who set the bow) be compelled by the judge to pay the entire wergeld according to the rank of the person to the relatives or master of him slain, according to the enactment of former laws.

[1] Cf. LXII.

XLVII

OF THE CONDEMNATION OF THIEVES, OF THEIR WIVES, AND OF
THEIR CHILDREN.

1. Although in former laws it has been established by what means
the crimes of robbers should be repressed, nevertheless, because
so far neither by corporal punishments nor by losses of property
has it been possible to bring an end to the cruel acts of robbers,
we decree in the present law: if any native freeman, barbarian as
well as Roman, or a person of any nation dwelling within the
provinces of our kingdom, takes horses or oxen in theft, and his wife
does not immediately reveal the committed crime, let her husband
be killed, and let her also be deprived of her liberty and given in
servitude without delay to him against whom the deed was committed; because it cannot be doubted, and is often discovered,
that such women are sharers in the crimes of their husbands.

2. Also regarding the children of such persons, let this punishment be followed according to law: if any of these at the time at
which the theft has been committed has passed the fourteenth
year of age, in accordance with the fact that the mother has been
condemned by previous judgment to the loss of her liberty, let him,
too, be placed in perpetual subjection under the dominion
(*dominium*) of that man against whom the theft is proved to have
been committed, since he knows about the committed crime beyond doubt if he has attained the stated number of years of
age.

3. However, those children of criminals who are found within the
tenth (fourteenth) [1] year of age at the time of the perpetrated
crime shall not be condemned to lose their liberty. Because just as
at such a tender age they do not have knowledge or understanding
of the crime committed by their father, so they cannot be blamed,
nor shall they sustain the previous judgment concerning their freedom; and the children who were innocent may claim the allotment of property (*sors*) and personal possessions (*facultas*) of
their parents.

[1] The best manuscripts give *decimum*. However, DeSalis has inserted *quar-
tum* to agree with XLII, 2.

4. Concerning the thefts and crimes of slaves, let that form of punishment be followed which is contained in the code of the ancient law.

XLVIII

OF INFLICTED WOUNDS.

1. If anyone resists violently in his own defense, let the rule be followed as established in former laws by what means he may be judged in the matter of wounds inflicted by the sword; but it is desirable to define in the present law matters omitted in this constitution relevant to later cases.

If therefore anyone breaks another's arm with a blow of stick or stone, and the injured man recovers the use of his limb without any permanent disability, let the doer of the deed be compelled to pay a tenth part of the wergeld, according to the status of the person, just as it is written in former laws.

2. Also if anyone strikes and breaks the shinbone of another by a similar accident, we order the same requirement to be observed in composition for the crime.

3. But if anyone's arm or shinbone has been broken in the above-mentioned manner, and he has suffered a clear disability, let that mode of composition be observed which has been decreed in former laws.

4. But if anyone resisting violently in his own cause and defense has committed acts of this sort from necessity, let him, even though he has departed unhurt, be compelled by order of the judge to pay half the established payment according to the degree of blame.

XLIX

OF ANIMALS CAUSING DAMAGE IN CLOSED FIELDS AND DRIVEN INTO ENCLOSURES, AND HORSES WANDERING AT LARGE.

1. This is established for the welfare and peace of all, that a general definition be set forth relevant to each and every case, so that the counts (*comites*) and magistrates (*praepositi*) of the localities, having been instructed adequately, may understand

more clearly how matters should be judged. If therefore anyone drives horses or oxen or any other animals of his fellow settlers (*vicini*) or those with whom they share property (*consortes*) which are doing damage to enclosures and shuts them up at his place, and if the mischance of fire occurs before he can send a messenger and bring immediate notice to their owner, let the man who shut them up pay half their value and let nothing further be demanded from him on this account.

2. Indeed, if animals which have been driven into an enclosure are taken in custody for a day and night, and he by whom they are held does not give notice to their owner or the manager of his property (*auctor*), and if afterward by some cause they die, let all those be replaced which were kept in custody without giving notice. But if the man to whom the animals belonged had been warned so that just as the law orders he might take them back after the extent of the damage caused by them had been estimated and he has delayed to do it through some undue lack of consideration, and if they suffer the mischance of death or injury while they are held within the enclosure, let him by whom they were retained suffer no loss or charge of blame nor be required to make any payment. We order the matter to be observed thus by the settlers (*vicini*) and those with whom they share property (*consortes*).

3. Concerning beasts of burden and animals that are wont to wander off, it is fitting that the general rule which has been established previously be observed, that is, that no one may seize another's horse wandering at large through the countryside. If anyone finds them doing damage to his property and shuts them up, let him institute a suit against his fellow settlers (*vicini*)[1] and those with whom they share property (*consortes*); and if their owner does not come (after the animals) let him (the plaintiff) drive them off his property in the presence of witnesses on the third day. But if anyone shall act otherwise and be convicted, let him be held liable to a triple compensation.

4. For a long time it has been displeasing to us that the law be admitted in which we ordered formerly that horses found and

---

[1] Here the word *vicini* seems to refer to the Burgundians while *consortes* refers to the Romans.

seized may be made the subject of legal contest and handed over to our servants (*pueri nostri*) [2] who collect fines in the districts so that they may be guarded with zeal and diligence by them. For we have noticed often and clearly that under the pretext of this law horses of various persons have been harmed rather than protected.

L

OF KILLING AGENTS OF THE KING AS WELL AS OF PRIVATE PERSONS.

1. However often cases of this kind come up in which the provisions of preceding constitutions have not clearly decreed what rules of procedure should be followed, it is necessary that an instruction be added to the laws indicating the means of ending the case, so that the judges of the various localities may fittingly terminate the suits, and so that delays due to ignorance may be eliminated.

Therefore we order that if any native free Burgundian or Roman who has clearly not been driven by necessity has killed an agent (steward) of our property, he shall be compelled to pay one hundred fifty solidi.

2. If he has killed the agent (steward) of another's property, let him pay one hundred solidi in composition for the crime.

3. Indeed if a slave of anyone without his master's knowledge kills an agent of our property or an agent of any other, just as it is established in other cases, let the slave be given over to death.

4. But if he has committed the crime of murder with his master's

---

[2] In the note to preface, 5, and that to Title XXXVIII, we have noted the existence of a number of royal officials termed variously as *proceres, optimates, comites, consilarii, domestici, majores domus regiae, cancellarii, notarii,* and *judices militantes.* There was another group of officials, possibly of inferior status, known as the *wittiscalci* or, as referred to in this law, *pueri nostri.* The *wittiscalci* (or the *pueri nostri*) were conspicuous among the royal servants since they acted as tax collectors for the *mulcta.* The word *wittiscalc* may be derived from *witte,* expressing the idea of a fine or penalty (*mulcta*) and *scalk* (Germ. *schalk*) which seems to mean a boy or slave. This compound indicates the meaning of a servant of the treasury (*mulcta*). Cf. Davoud-Oghlou, *op. cit.,* I, 134–35, 445. Also cf. LXXVI.

knowledge, let the slave die after he has been presented to the judge. Furthermore, let his master be compelled to pay the entire wergeld of the man killed, and in addition let him be compelled to pay a fine of twelve solidi.

5. Also if anyone who has been injured by blows or wounds kills one of our agents (stewards) or the agent (steward) of a private individual, and this is clearly proved, let that form of satisfaction be observed which earlier statutes have ordered.

LI

OF THOSE WHO DO NOT GIVE THEIR SONS THE PORTIONS OF THEIR PROPERTY DUE TO THEM.

1. Although these things have been observed from of old among our people, that a father should divide his property equally by law among his sons, nevertheless we have ordered in a law established now for a long time that this practice be observed, and we have added this useful counsel to fathers that a father should have freedom to do what he wishes with that which belongs to his own portion.

But because in a recent controversy it became clear that a certain Athila had passed over the provisions of the old enactments and displayed insubordination to these most useful precepts of law and had not given his son the portion due to him but had transferred his property to other persons through illegal written title since he had wished nothing therefrom to belong to his son, and that no one may follow a bad example in this manner, we order that what he has done contrary to law shall have no legal force, and we add that all his property shall be possessed by his son. It is also the purpose of our judgment to cut off the disobedience of the transgressor, so that the justice of the general precept will be inscribed in the laws and retained.

On this account we have ordered in matters of this sort that the law be observed which was promulgated long ago to the effect that any man who will not hand over portions of his property legally belonging to his sons may do nothing adverse or prejudicial to them in writing, and if he does so, it shall be invalid.

2. Nevertheless, it is pleasing that this rule be defined thus with

the force of law, that a son shall have full power of doing what he wishes with the portion he receives, with the further provision that if he dies without heirs and the decrees of fate permit his father to survive, and if he has made no gift from the property legally belonging to him during his lifetime and left no will, then his father may claim the succession to these portions in question. However, the father shall have no power of alienating them and when he has died the property of their dead brother will pass to the remaining sons.

3. The mother's ornaments and vestments belong to the daughters without any right to share on the part of the brother or brothers; further, let this legal principle be observed concerning those ornaments and vestments in the case of girls whose mothers die intestate. But if the mother shall have made any disposal of her own ornaments and vestments, there shall be no cause for action thereafter.

4. But if an unmarried girl who has sisters dies, and she has not declared her wish in writing or in the presence of witnesses, let her portion after her death belong to her sisters and, as has been stated, let her brothers have no share therein.

5. However if the girl dies and does not have a blood sister, and no clear disposition has been made concerning her property, let her brothers become her heirs.

LII

OF BETROTHED WOMEN WHO, INCITED BY DESIRE, GO TO CONSORT WITH OTHERS.

1. Howsoever often such cases arise concerning which none of the preceding laws have established provisions, it is fitting that the ambiguity of the matter be removed so that the judgment set forth shall receive the strength of perpetual law, and the special case shall have general application.

2. Since the deserts of a criminal case which is pending between Fredegisil, our sword-bearer on the one side, and Balthamodus together with Aunegild on the other, have been heard and considered, we give an opinion which punishes this recent crime and imposes a method of restraint for the future.

3. And since Aunegild, after the death of her first husband, retaining her own legal competence, promised herself, not only with the consent of her parents, but also with her own desire and will, to the above-mentioned Fredegisil, and since she had received the greater part of the wedding price which her betrothed had paid, she broke her pledged faith, having been aroused by the ardor of her desire for Balthamodus. Furthermore, she not only violated her vows, but repeated her customary shameful union, and on account of this, she ought to atone for such a crime and such a violation of her free status not otherwise than with the pouring forth of her own blood. Nevertheless we command, placing reverence for these holy days before public punishment, that Aunegild, deprived of honor by human and divine judgment, should pay her wergeld, that is three hundred solidi, to Fredegisil under compulsion.

4. Nor do we remove merited condemnation from Balthamodus who presumed to receive a woman due in marriage to another man, for his case deserves death. But in consideration of the holy days, we recall our sentence for his execution, under the condition that he should be compelled to pay his wergeld of one hundred fifty solidi to that Fredegisil unless he offers evident (public) oaths with eleven others in which he affirms that at that time in which he was united with the above-mentioned Aunegild as if by the right of marriage, he was unaware that she was pledged to Fredegisil. But if he shall have so sworn, let him suffer neither loss nor punishment.

5. In truth we command that the judgment set forth in this case be established to remain the law forever, and lest the moderation of the composition now permitted encourage anyone hereafter to commit a deed of such great crime, we command that whosoever incurs the guilt of such a deed not only may sustain the loss of his property, but also may be punished by the loss of his life. For it is preferable that the multitude be corrected by the condemnation of a few rather than that the appearance of unsuitable moderation introduce a pretext which may contribute to the license of delinquency.

Given on the 29th of March (517) at Lyons, Agapitus being consul.

LIII

Of the Inheritance of Sons Who, After the Death of Their Father, Die Intestate, While Their Mother Still Survives.

1. It has been permitted now for a long time as set forth and established in previous law, that if, a father being dead, his son dies without a will and the mother still lives, she shall possess the substance (usufruct) of the son's property during the rest of her life, and after her death the nearest relatives of the son coming from the father's side shall receive all those properties of which we speak. However, discussing this case more thoroughly with the nobles of our people (*obtimates populi nostri*), we direct attention to the fact that the nature of this afore-mentioned law causes no less of loss and discord than of advantage to the heirs since they disagree among themselves over the various contradictions involved in the contest. As a result, on the one hand, the slowness of acquiring inheritance gives offense, and on the other the loss of property causes anxiety. Therefore it seems more just that the bonds of the above-mentioned condition should be relaxed under circumstances whereby the case will not be delayed, but ended.

2. Therefore we order, that, just as a similar case was concluded by our decision, since the contrary decrees of the fates often shift under these circumstances, a legal division of the remaining property shall be made on an equal basis immediately between the mother of the deceased son, if there be no daughter, and his nearest relatives as we mentioned above, with the further provision that each of them may have the power according to law of doing what he pleases with the half received. For surely it is more desirable that the cases should terminate immediately to the welfare of the parties concerned rather than that anyone should gain an advantage because of any delay in point of time.

LIV

OF THOSE WHO PRESUME TO TAKE A THIRD OF THE SLAVES AND
TWO PARTS OF THE LAND (OF THEIR HOST) CONTRARY TO PUBLIC
PROHIBITION.[1]

1. It was commanded at the time the order was issued whereby
our people should receive one-third of the slaves, and two-thirds
of the land, that whoever had received land together with slaves
either by the gift of our predecessors or of ourselves, should not
require a third of the slaves nor two parts of the land from that
place in which hospitality had been assigned him; nevertheless inasmuch as we find many unmindful of their danger because they
have taken in excess of those things which we have ordered, it is
necessary that the present authority issued in the image of eternal
law coerce the presumptuous and provide a remedy of due security
against these acts of contempt. We order then that whatever lands
have been taken contrary to our official prohibition from their
hosts by those who already have possession of fields and slaves
through our gift shall be restored without delay.

2. Also concerning clearings, we order that the new and unjust
strife and trickery of the *faramanni* [2] which causes anxiety and dis-

---

[1] This is a reference to hospitality in the more technical sense. The barbarians who were allowed to enter the Empire as *foederati* were established
on the land by a system of hospitality which was based on the old Roman
precedent of quartering soldiers on the land, allowing them one-third of the
property of the original owner. Between the Burgundians and the Romans,
it seems that the Burgundians took one-third of the slaves and two-thirds of
the land of the host to whom they had been assigned; perhaps this particular
arrangement was made because the Burgundians had brought some slaves
with them—barbarians of other nations who had been captured in battle—
and had no need for as many as half of the Roman slaves. Upon the matter of
royal gifts of land and the conditions under which it was held, see I, 4.

[2] The word *faramanni* is a disputed one and has been explained in several
ways. A meaning connected with the German word *fahren* has been suggested—that the *faramanni* were *coloni* or enfranchised slaves who had been
given permission by their master to go (*fahren*) where they pleased. Again,
faramanni has been explained as those Burgundians who arrived later, that
is, after the first division of the land had been made, and so claimed the
right to divide property with a Roman who had remained without a guest at
the first division. Cf. Davoud-Oghlou, *op. cit.*, I, 433, n. 2. DuCange suggests
a slightly different meaning derived from the relation of the word *faramanni*
to *fara* (*generatio*) and *man* (*homo*), based upon the fact that the word here

quiet to the possessors be suppressed by this law, with the result that, just as concerning forests, so also concerning clearings made either heretofore or at the present time, the Roman possessors shall have a share with the Burgundians, for, as was established previously, we order half of the forests in general to belong to the Romans; likewise concerning courtyards and orchards, let this condition be followed among the *faramanni,* that is, that the Romans may lay claim to take half the property.[3]

3. But if anyone exceeds the established provisions of this law and is not reprimanded and punished by you, do not doubt that the fervor of our wrath will be aroused to your peril.

LV

OF EXCLUDING BARBARIANS WHENEVER CONTENTION ARISES BETWEEN TWO ROMANS CONCERNING THE BOUNDARIES OF THEIR FIELDS.[1]

1. Inasmuch as it has been established under certain penalty that no barbarian should dare to involve himself in a suit which a Roman has brought against another Roman, we advocate a stricter handling of these cases, and command that the law remain just as we ordered it established in earlier times.

2. As often as cases arise between two Romans concerning the boundaries of fields which are possessed by barbarians through

is opposed to the Romans; hence the *faramanni* were those to whom hospitality had been assigned, that is, they were heads of families (DuCange, *op. cit.,* III, 204-5). This latter is the explanation accepted also by Dahn. *Faramanni* is a Burgundian and Lombard word compounded out of *Fara (Geschlecht, Sippe),* and *Mann,* i.e., the *faramanni* were *Sippe-Häupter, Hausväter,* the heads of households who held land. This would explain *faramanni* as simply those Burgundians who held land as opposed to the original Roman possessors. Cf. Felix Dahn, *Die Könige der Germanen,* XI, 62–63. Cf. *Lex Langobardorum, Rotharis leges,* 117, and *Lex Anglo-Saxonum, Aethelstanes domas, Concilium Exoniense,* Preface (Davoud-Oghlou, *op. cit.,* II, 21–22, 511).

[3] The phrase "the Romans may lay claim to take half the property" is an attempt to translate the phrase *ut medietatem Romani estiment praesumendam.* Beyerle avoids the difficulty by taking the phrase as *ut de medietate Romani nihil estiment praesumendam* (A 4, B 2–10) which would render a translation something like "they shall not lay claim to the half belonging to the Roman." Cf. Beyerle, *op. cit.,* p. 86; DeSalis, *op. cit.,* p. 89.

[1] Cf. XXII.

the law of hospitality, let the guests of the contestants not be involved in the quarrel, but let them await the outcome between the Romans contending in judgment. And the guest of the victor shall have a share of the property obtained as a result of his success.

3. But if any barbarian involves himself in a litigation of this kind and is defeated, let him pay a fine of twelve solidi for holding this law in contempt.

4. But if a Roman presumes to engage him who is his guest in litigation, we order both to pay twelve solidi, and the case to be settled by Roman law.

5. But if a contention has been raised concerning the boundaries of a field which a barbarian has received intact with slaves by public gift, it is permitted him to settle the case by Roman law whether it is brought against him or he himself has instigated it.

6. Further, if a native freeman presumes to remove or destroy a boundary marker, let him be condemned to the loss of a hand. If a slave has done this, let him be killed.

7. If indeed a native freeman wishes to redeem (avert) this mutilating punishment, let him pay half his wergeld.

LVI

Of Slaves Bought in Alamannia.

1. If anyone buys back another's slave in Alamannia, either let his master pay his price (wergeld) or let him who redeems him have the slave; furthermore we order this to be observed henceforth from the present time.

2. Also if a native freeman has been redeemed at his own request, let him return his price (wergeld) to the buyer.

LVII

Of Freedmen of the Burgundians Who Do Not Have the Privilege of Departing.

A freedman of a Burgundian who has not given his master twelve solidi as is the custom so that he may have the privilege of departing whither he wishes, and who has not received his third [1] from the Romans (i.e., from the Roman property owners) must be treated as a member of his master's household.

LVIII

OF KILLING DOGS.

If anyone kills a dog without any apparent cause, let him give a solidus to him to whom the dog belonged.

LIX

OF GRANDCHILDREN.

If the father is dead, let a grandchild with all his possessions be given over to the supervision and care of the grandfather if his mother has decided upon a second marriage. Moreover, if she fails to remarry because she has chosen chastity, let her children with all their property remain in her care (custody) and power.

LX

OF EMPLOYING WITNESSES OF GIFTS.

1. Since the ancient custom is often neglected in various legal matters, it is necessary that consideration be taken for future times through a new law. And because we know some barbarians are willing, with two or three witnesses present, to take possession of property in the name of gift or inheritance contrary to the ancient custom, we have first corrected their presumption by the present law, decreeing that property is not validly transmitted by means of so few witnesses (i.e., that a matter confirmed by so few witnesses is invalid).

2. Moreover, if hereafter any barbarian wishes to make a will (*testari*) or gift (*donare*), either the Roman or the barbarian custom must be observed if he wishes his action to have any validity, that is, either let what he wishes to give to anyone be

---

[1] Cf. DeSalis, *op. cit.*, p. 91, n. 3, for *tertram*. Evidently "third" refers to a third portion of the land. Perhaps this is the amount which the system of hospitality observed among the Burgundians would assign to a freedman.

confirmed by legal written documents, or at any rate, let what he wishes to bestow or give obtain validity from the witness of five native freemen, and let the property be transferred to the jurisdiction of him to whom it has been granted.

3. If a sufficient number of native freemen is not present, we permit freedmen to render testimony. And among the native freemen, it is fitting that a number of our (royal) slaves be admitted (to give testimony), provided that witnesses are pledged (bound) by the hand (*manus*) of him who wishes to give or transfer anything, or if a question is raised regarding the trustworthiness of a witness, according to the custom of the barbarians, let him take oath.

LXI

Of Women Who Willingly Seek Union with a Man.[1]

Whatever woman, barbarian by nation, enters into union with a man willingly and secretly, let her wedding price be paid in fee simple to her relatives; and he to whom she has been joined in an adulterous union may be united afterward in marriage to another if he wishes.

LXII

Of Only Sons.

1. Let an only son, if his father is dead, leave a third part of his property for the use of his mother, provided nevertheless she does not take another husband; for if she enters another marriage, let her lose all.

2. Nevertheless, let her use her wedding gift (*dos*) [1] which she received from her husband, as long as she lives, and let the ownership be reserved for the son.

Given on the tenth day of June, in the second year of our lord the king (517).

---

[1] Cf. XII, 3.

---

[1] Cf. LXVI.

LXIII

OF THOSE WHO HAVE STOLEN GRAIN STANDING IN SHEAVES (*in Gremiis*).

If a native freeman has taken grain which is standing in sheaves, let him pay threefold, and let the fine be according to the rank of the person. If a slave has done so, let his master pay in simple for him, and let the slave receive three hundred blows.

LXIV

OF ANIMALS KILLED IN THE HARVEST.

1. If anyone has killed an animal in his harvest, let him first be paid the damage which the animal has caused, and let him return the animal (or perhaps the value of the animal) which he killed.
2. This is to be observed concerning larger animals.
3. Moreover concerning smaller animals, let it be observed as has been established in an earlier law.[1]

LXV

OF WIDOWS FROM WHOM THE DEBTS OF THEIR HUSBANDS ARE SOUGHT.

1. If any widow has sons, and if she and her sons have made a cession of the goods of the deceased husband, let them suffer no suit for recovery nor further claim on account of his debts.
2. If indeed they assume the inheritance, let them also pay the paternal debt.

LXVI

OF GIRLS WITHOUT FATHERS AND MOTHERS WHO ARE GIVEN IN MARRIAGE.

1. If a girl is given in marriage and has neither father nor brothers, but only an uncle and sisters, let the uncle receive a third part of the *wittimon,* and let the sisters know they may claim another third.

[1] Cf. XXIII, 5.

2. If indeed she is without father or brothers, and she receives a husband, it is pleasing that the mother receive a third part of the *wittimon,* and the nearest relatives another third.

3. If she does not have a mother, let her sisters receive that third.[1]

LXVII

This Must Be Observed Concerning Forests.

If any persons have cultivated fields of their own or lands tilled by serfs, let them know the forest must be divided among them according to the extent of their holdings and the proportion of the total in their possession; nevertheless let half the clearings in the forests be left for the Romans.[1]

LXVIII

Of Adultery.

1. If adulterers are discovered, let the man and woman be killed.

2. This must be observed: either let him (the injured party) kill both of them, or if he kills only one of them, let him pay the wergeld of that one according to that customary wergeld which has been established in earlier laws.

LXIX

Of the Wedding Gift (*Wittimon*).

1. If a woman enters upon a second marriage, let her *wittimon* be claimed by the nearest relatives of the first husband.

2. If indeed she wishes to take a third husband, let the *wittimon* which the husband gives go to the woman.

LXX

Of Thefts.

1. If a native freeman and a slave commit a theft together, let the freeman pay triple the value of what was stolen, provided it was

---

[1] These laws seem to account for two-thirds of the *wittimon.* Could the other third be the girl's wedding gift or portion? Cf. LXII, 2; LXXXVI, 2.

---

[1] Cf. LIV, 2.

not a capital crime; further let the slave be flogged as a punishment.[1]

2. Indeed if it is a case in which we order a man to be killed, and if he has fled into a church, let him redeem himself according to the amount established by him from whom he stole, and let him pay a fine of twelve solidi.

3. If however it is a minor theft, that is, if he has stolen a pig, a sheep, a goat, or a hive of bees, let him pay a fine of three solidi.

4. If he commits violence, let the amount of the fine be six solidi.

LXXI

Of Those Who Compound a Theft.

1. If anyone believes that a theft which has been committed may be compounded without the knowledge of the judges, let him receive the punishment to which a thief would be subjected.

2. If anyone assuming the place of a judge wishes to set the composition between the above-mentioned parties, let him pay a fine of twelve solidi.

LXXII

Of Traps for Animals.[1]

If anyone sets a trap for wild animals outside the cultivated land, and places it in a deserted spot, and by chance, a man or animal runs into it, no blame shall be attributed to him who owned the trap on this account.

LXXIII

Of Horses Which Have Bones and Sticks (*Scindola*) Tied to Their Tails.

1. If an animal shall have been found in that place in which it causes loss, or outside as well, and if it shall have been endangered

[1] Cf. XCI.

---

[1] Cf. XLVI.

or killed or injured because of fear (of the *scindola*),[1] let it be in the power of the owner of the animal to decide whether he wishes to receive it back together with another, or if he does not want to take back his own, let him give an estimate of its value, and we order that two such horses be given to the owner by him who, contrary to our order, presumes to do such things; we order that freemen be held liable for punishment in accordance with this law.

2. Moreover, if a slave presumes to do this, let him receive two hundred blows, and let it be in the power of the owner of the horse to take back the horse if he wishes. But if the animal is displeasing to him (i.e., if the owner does not wish to take back his horse), observe the rule as has been stated concerning the punishment of a slave, and let the master of the slave be compelled to return a horse of the same value to him who owned the injured horse. Likewise let it be observed in the case of a mare.

3. In the case of a horse whose tail has been clipped, let a similar punishment be imposed.

LXXIV

Of Widows and Their Children.

1. Indeed it has been established in general in a law stated in earlier times that if a woman whose husband has died childless

---

[1] This law is an example of what seems to have been a fairly common practice with the lawmakers of the Code: the offense itself is stated in the title of the law only, while the body of the law deals with the punishment to be imposed and certain modifications. This law seems to say that if anyone finds an animal in his field and if, in order to scare it off or to obtain revenge upon its master for allowing it to stray, he ties bones or sticks to its tail in such a manner that it disconcerts or frightens the animal so that it runs wildly about and is injured or killed, then he who was guilty of tying the sticks to the animal's tail must return that animal together with another like it to its master, or if the animal is so injured that the master does not wish to receive it back, then the guilty party must return two like animals to the master. This law seems very barbarous in comparison with the bulk of the laws contained in the Code, but it does not seem to be out of keeping with such laws as XCVII and XCVIII. Moreover, since it seems unlikely that the Burgundians could have adopted such a completely Romanized life as is portrayed in the major portion of the laws in such a short time as they had been within the Empire, it may be that these more "primitive" laws give us a more accurate picture of Burgundian society as it actually was than the more sophisticated Roman-like laws.

does not enter into a second marriage, she may claim a third of his inheritance for her own use throughout her lifetime [1]; but now after considering more carefully with the nobles (*obtimates*) of our people all these matters set forth under this same title, it pleases us to limit the general application of the above-mentioned law.

Wherefore we order that any such widow, concerning whom we speak, may receive a portion of the inheritance of her husband if she has not already obtained property from her father or mother, or if her husband has not given her any portion of his property by means of which she can live.

2. If any woman whose husband has died does not take vows to a second husband, or does not wish her sons, now grown, to live with her, she may accordingly divide the property of the dead husband with them. If she has one son only, let her obtain the above-mentioned third; if there are two or three or four or more sons, let her receive a fourth part; nevertheless after her death, let the property return to the sons.

3. If anyone enters a second marriage after the death of his first wife by whom he had children, and has children also by this second wife, and if he then dies, the rule should be observed that his widow shall not hold that anything must be given to her from the portion of her stepchildren, but let her receive the portion designated above from the property inherited by her own children.[2]

LXXV

OF AN INHERITANCE DIVIDED BETWEEN NEPHEW AND AUNT.

1. It is fitting that those suits which are not shown to have been regulated by prior decrees should be settled by the equity of a newly stated (*prolatae*) law, so that the heirs may not remain ignorant of the order of procedure in this present matter of the succession, and so that a competent instruction for judges may not be lacking.

Therefore if a son whose father is still living has a son, and if he (the son) dies leaving a sister, the father just mentioned should bestow the portion of his property due to his son in this manner. From that amount of property which belongs to him at his own

---

[1] Cf. XLII, 1.
[2] Cf. I, 2.

death (i.e., from that half of the entire property which he retained for himself after dividing with his son), he shall make no special bequest to grandson and daughter, but half shall be kept for the portion of the minor party [1] from the paternal inheritance, while the other half of the property shall be divided equally between the grandson and daughter (who stand in the relation to one another of nephew and aunt).

2. But if the son with whose posterity this law deals shall possess all things undivided with his father, on his death let one half go to the portion of the grandson, while the other half should be divided in equal parts between the daughter and grandson.[2]

3. And that no motive of litigation may be left unremoved from this same title, whether there are one or two or more daughters, we command that the statement of law be observed which we set forth above, that is, that half (of the undivided property left after the grandson had received half, i.e., his father's share, of the total) be acquired by the daughters, half by the grandson or grandsons from the son.

4. If indeed as has been said, the father has died, and the son leaves no male heirs, but a daughter only, and the sisters of her father (i.e., the above son) are still living, the law establishes the rule for claiming the title of inheritance as follows: the amount of the father's portion must be set aside (for the daughter), while the other half (i.e., her grandfather's portion) shall legally belong to

---

[1] Beyerle, *op. cit.*, p. 103, n. 1, suggests that the minor party is one not yet of age, i.e., the daughter. It is hard to see how *minor persona* would necessarily mean daughter unless it means "not enjoying full legal competence." Whatever the explanation given, it seems that *minor persona* must refer to the daughter since according to LXXVIII, 2, the portion which a father retained for himself after the division with his sons might be left only to the surviving sons, the grandsons might not succeed to that share. In our present law, only a daughter and a grandson survive. It would seem that the daughter, as the only direct heir of her father, should receive the greater part of that half of the entire property which the father had retained for himself; if we regard the *minor persona* as the daughter, then the daughter would receive three-fourths and the grandson one-fourth of that half of the property which the father retained for his own use.

[2] This section of the law deals with the entire property since the father and son had not made a division. In this case, the grandson gets three-fourths of the entire property, the daughter one-fourth (whereas above where the property had been divided before the father's death, she received three-eighths of the entire property).

the aunts mentioned above, nor let it be thought that any of their half may be claimed by the daughter (the only heir of the son).

LXXVI

OF ROYAL SERVANTS (*Wittiscalci*).[1]

1. The complaint is made constantly by our counts (*comites*) that some of our people have become so presumptuous that they have struck down our servants (*pueri nostri*) who execute our judgments and collect fines at our command, and have not hesitated to seize by force the pledges given by the order of the counts.

Because of such acts we decree in the present law that if anyone hereafter strikes down our servants (*pueri nostri*) or removes pledges insolently, and these facts are established upon investigation by order of a judge, he shall be held liable to a triple satisfaction, that is, he who did violence will be compelled to pay three solidi for a blow for which a single solidus would be paid ordinarily.

2. And also those things which were removed by violence shall be returned with a thrice ninefold payment [2]; with the further provision that such presumptuous persons must pay the fine owed to us.

3. Also women will likewise be held to the payment of the fine if they treat our servants (*wittiscalci*) with contempt.

4. Now we wish this stated form of punishment to be observed then, that our servants (*pueri nostri*), mindful of their danger, will take care not to exceed their orders presumptuously in any case whatsoever. We have ordered that injuries committed by them be avenged, so that they may have no doubt that punishment will ensue unless they observe with all diligence those orders which have been given them.

Given on the 27th of June (513), in the consulship of Probus, *vir clarissimus*.

---

[1] Cf. XLIX, 4, n. 2.

[2] This excessive payment might be explained by the fact that it is imposed on those who hold the royal representatives and their commands in contempt. Cf. *Lex Alamannorum*, VII, 1, which imposes a comparable penalty, *tres novigeldos*, for theft from a church.

LXXVII

Of Warrants (*Inscriptiones*).[1]

1. However often a slave is accused of crime and however often it is necessary that he be handed over to the judge under a warrant, this procedure in holding an examination shall be observed, namely, that the value of the slave shall be paid to his master; and if the slave has confessed under torture the crime of which he has been accused, let the solidi which were put up as the value of the slave be paid back to the accusing parties, and let the slave be condemned to a deserved death. After this has been done, let the master of the criminal slave make restitution in fee simple by law to him who lost the property so that he may be without loss.

2. Indeed if he has been placed under torture and has not been convicted and has not confessed, let the master retain the money paid as the slave's price; and let him receive back the innocent slave.

3. We have found through the statements of many persons what customs and procedure have been observed among our people heretofore, namely, that (an equal) contribution by each party should constitute the reward which is promised and paid for evidence in any theft or crime. And therefore it seems right that when the existing inapplicable law has been removed, if a native freeman is convicted on charges of this kind, let him sustain the entire expense for the penalty and evidence according to law. Thus we may act without prejudice to previous laws which have been established for repressing the crimes of slaves.

LXXVIII

Of the Succession of Inheritance.

1. Upon careful consideration of these matters, we have established that if a father shall have divided his allotment (*sors*) with his sons and afterward it happens a son dies childless while his father is still living, the father may claim the use of the entire

[1] Cf. VII.

portion by the law of usufruct in accordance with the son's wish. But upon the father's death, let him divide between sons and grandsons so that all fatherless grandsons sprung from any one son shall obtain such a portion as their father would have had.

2. Further, let that portion which the father had retained (for himself after the) division among his sons be left to the surviving sons, and let the grandsons not succeed to that share.

3. Nevertheless the present law pertains to male heirs only.

LXXIX

Of Prescription (i.e., the Setting of Time Limits or the Establishment of Title).

1. Now for a long time it has been ordained by us that if anyone of our people has invited a person belonging to a barbarian nation to live with him, and if he has voluntarily given him land to dwell upon, and he (the one to whom the land was given) has held it for fifteen years without prohibition,[1] let it remain in his possession (potestas). And let him who made the gift know that nothing shall be paid to him therefor. Furthermore, it pleases us to establish by the present law that this well-known condition ought to be observed generally without any change through all time.

2. If anyone claims and it is proved that land was taken by force by another, and if it is established that the property was appropriated, before thirty years have been completed it can be recovered and restored to the parties seeking its return.

3. Moreover, if thirty years have been completed and the land has not been restored, even though the claim is made that it was seized, let the claimant know that none of it need be returned to him.

4. Wherefore all counts (comites), whenever contention shall arise from the afore-mentioned causes, should take care to render decisions justly according to the provision of this law.

5. And because it is fitting that all things pertaining to the peace of all be provided by law, we desire that all claims concerning any property whatsoever which shall not have been completed

---

[1] For this unusual meaning of the verb testare implying prohibition, cf. DuCange, op. cit., VI, 565.

within thirty years, shall not be affected thereafter by any order, because the number of years established above is sufficient time for everyone to demand and recover what is due him.

Given on the 1st of March (515) at Lyons, in the consulship of Senator, *vir clarissimus,* consul.

LXXX

OF THOSE BEARING FALSE WITNESS AND FALSE ACCUSERS (SLANDERERS).

1. As new cases appear, it is necessary that those things which have not been well-defined should be established with the sanction of current law. Because we know many have sworn falsely in different cases on account of its ease who afterward expose themselves voluntarily to combat so that they may prove (establish) their statements when they fear for their own loss, we issue this order concerning witnesses:

2. If those who bear witness for any party resort to combat to decide the case, and, by divine judgment, the false witness falls in the struggle, let all the witnesses of that party whose testimony was disproved be compelled to pay a fine of three hundred solidi at the place. For we believe that the crime of many bearing witness falsely cannot be expiated by the death of one, so we have established that those whom fortune does not punish shall suffer loss as a punishment so that hereafter no one may readily dare to lie in accordance with his own depraved nature.

3. Also if anyone has given counsel to a false accuser with regard to undertaking combat (i.e., has instigated a false accuser to give combat), and if he has been defeated, let him pay a fine like that which has been stated above.

LXXXI

OF FUTURE APPEALS BEFORE JUDGES.

1. In the introductory statute (*prima constitutio*), it was decreed by us that judges, after a third appeal, should settle and decide cases between the recognized parties, and since it is clear that the assigned judges are frequently occupied or absent at the time of appeal, we believe a time should be established with the consent of all [1] so that a judge who has entertained an appeal (three times) during a period of three months may not be permitted to delay any case further unless for the purpose of obtaining fuller knowledge, and so that when judgment is given he may decide all things in such a manner that nothing remains in doubt between the parties.

2. If the judges have entertained an appeal beyond three months in a recognized case and failed to render judgment, we order them to pay a fine of twelve solidi, and the case nonetheless is to be decided by these laws.

LXXXII

OF GUARANTORS (OATHTAKERS).

1. If anyone accepts a guarantor (oathtaker) at a hearing, let the guarantor (oathtaker) insist on clearing himself (establishing his integrity) so that the case may proceed.

2. But if the guarantor (oathtaker) has died, let the heirs of the dead man appeal to the judge of the locality, and let the adversary be compelled by his order to accept another guarantor (oathtaker) of the same legal competence, and let nothing be sought from the heirs of the dead guarantor (oathtaker).

LXXXIII

OF THOSE WHO IDENTIFY THEIR PROPERTY IN THE POSSESSION OF OTHERS.

1. Whoever identifies his property, whether bondservant or anything else that is his, shall receive a satisfactory guarantor (oath-

---

[1] "and since it is clear that the assigned judges are frequently occupied or absent at the time of appeal, we believe a time should be established with the consent of all . . ." translates DeSalis' text: *et quia occupationes et absentias deputatorum iudicum frequenter patuit evenire expetitione, consensu omnium tempus credidimus statuendum* . . . However Beyerle substitutes the reading: *et quia occupationes et absentias deputatorum iudicum frequenter patuit evenire, ex petitione ac consensu omnium tempus credidimus statuendum* . . . which he translates: *Weil aber die bestallten Richter scheinbar (sonstwie) oft beansprucht oder auswärts sind, glaubten Wir auf Bitten (und) mit Beifall aller eine (feste) Frist ansetzen zu sollen:* "But since the assigned judges are often occupied or absent, we believe a time should be set at the request and with the consent of all." Evidently the readings of the manuscripts are so varied it is impossible to establish an authoritative text at all. Cf. Beyerle, *op. cit.,* p. 110, n. 1; and DeSalis, *op. cit.,* p. 105.

taker) from the possessor, and if he does not receive the guarantor (oathtaker) desired, let him have the right of taking the thing which he identified.

2. If indeed he has been mistaken in identification, let him be compelled to restore the article which he identified falsely, as well as another of like value.

3. If a slave identifies falsely, let him be beaten according to the value of the thing identified.

LXXXIV

Of the Sale of Lands.

1. Because we know that the Burgundian allotments have been sold away (dissipated) with too much ease, we believe this rule should be established in the present law, that no one is permitted to sell his land unless he has an allotment or possessions in another place.

2. Also let this prohibition be added, that if anyone who has land elsewhere needs to sell it, then no outsider (*extraneus*) shall be set over (preferred to) a Roman host in the purchase of any property which a Burgundian has for sale, nor shall an outsider be permitted to buy land under any pretext.

3. Furthermore, it must be observed that his host may buy from him only who is proved to hold land elsewhere.

LXXXV

Of Wards.[1]

1. If a mother wishes to assume guardianship (*tutela*),[2] no other relationship (*parentela*) shall be placed before her.

---

[1] Cf. LIX.

[2] The ideas conveyed by the expressions *tutela* and *parentela* are legal abstractions based on the principle of family control of individual relationship within the group. *Parentela* involves recognition of the powers and duties attached to parenthood including the personal relation of parental supervision and control, whereas *tutela* implies the powers of protection and guardianship associated with a ward, and predominantly affects the property rather than the person of the ward. The principle of *parentela* places an individual under the legal jurisdiction of the father or other family head (*alieni juris*) as derived from *patria potestas*, but *tutela* is admitted only in cases of persons who

2. But if indeed there is no mother, then the nearest relative shall assume the property of the minor under the condition that to the degree that his own property is increased, the property of the minor should also be increased to his advantage; nor is it permitted to waste or alienate any of it.

3. If indeed anyone presumes to take any of the property of minors, as has been said, let him return it in simple from his own property; also if a minor party is involved in a suit, let that person answer who has his wardship.

LXXXVI

Of the Marriage Ornaments (*Malahereda*).

1. If a father leaves daughters, and while living, wishes to give the marriage ornaments (*malahereda*), let him give to whom he pleases, with the consequence that no one may seek their return to his daughters.

2. If the father shall have asked that the marriage portion (*wittimon*) not be sought, let his wish be disregarded; but, as a former law has stated, let the nearest relative receive it [1]; with the further provision that the girl will obtain a third part of the ornaments (of the marriage portion) which the relative has received.

LXXXVII

Of Contracts Entered into by Minors.

1. We believe that the following provision should be made concerning the age of minors (for their protection), that they shall

---

are *sui juris*. "Its intention is to give to persons otherwise capable of legal acts, but of weak age or sex, protection from the consequences of acts by which they would, but for such protection, be bound. Persons *alieni juris*, a slave, a son or a daughter, are essentially incapable of legal acts binding on themselves, and the notion of protection in their exercise becomes absurd. Thus the conditions under which these two relations exist are mutually exclusive." J. L. Strachan-Davidson, *Problems of the Roman Criminal Law*, I, 33.

---

[1] Perhaps this means that if a father, before his death, requests that his heirs not seek a *wittimon* in case of the marriage of one of his daughters, that that request should be ignored and the provisions of LXVI—that the relatives should receive two-thirds of it and the girl one-third as her marriage portion —be followed.

not be permitted to have the liberty of making sales or bequests before fifteen years of age. And if they have been cheated because of their infancy, let none of it be valid. Thus what they have done before the fifteenth year of age, they may have the power of retracting within another fifteen years if they wish.

2. But if they have not retracted it within the stated time, let it be permanent and remain valid.

LXXXVIII

Of Emancipation.

Since the title of emancipation takes precedence over the law of possession, great care must be exercised in such matters. And therefore it should be observed, that if anyone wishes to manumit a slave, he may do so by giving him his liberty through a legally competent document; or if anyone wishes to give freedom to a bondservant without a written document, let the manumission thus conferred be confirmed with the witness of not less than five or seven native freemen, because it is not fitting to present a smaller number of witnesses than is required when the manumission is in written form.

CONTINUATION OF THE BOOK OF CONSTITUTIONS

LXXXIX

Of Animals Which Have Entered a Vineyard.

1. Inasmuch as we are concerned with the pursuit and useful purpose of agriculture, a general complaint has been brought to us not only regarding our lands, but also the lands of other proprietors, charging that vineyards are guarded in many places with such negligence that they are ruined constantly by cattle and other animals. As a result, either the vines themselves are torn and cut off by grazing animals or, trodden and broken from the ground itself, they are pulled up by the roots, whence the edict of our father of glorious memory was issued in former times regarding the killing of each and every such animal or rendering compensation therefor. However, we recognize that this has not been observed owing to the negligence of all.

2. Therefore we order that at whatever time smaller animals, that is, goats, sheep, or pigs, are found in a vineyard, one may be selected from among them, as often as they are found, and then killed and kept by the master of the vineyard.

3. If indeed, after a third warning, a cow is found in a vineyard, it may be killed likewise and kept by the master of the vineyard.

4. Indeed, in the case of oxen, work horses, asses, or riding horses,[1] we order that if the above-mentioned animals have been found, the master or custodian of the vineyard may shut them up; and let their owner pay a single tremissis to him who holds them in custody.

5. If, indeed, a native freeman presumes rashly to take them from the enclosure, let him be fined in the amount of six solidi; if a slave has done this, let him receive two hundred blows after he has been delivered up by his master.

6. If indeed either the owner or his herdsman does not wish to redeem animals held in an enclosure within two days and in any wise make the above-mentioned payment, or if the steward or master does not impose a punishment of two hundred blows on the slave, we order that the above-mentioned payment be directed by the judge, or in the absence of a judge, by his subordinate (*praepositus*) to the owner of the vineyard.

We order that this decree and command be proclaimed among our laws regarding the execution of penalties since it is suited to the general welfare.

XC

OF JUDGMENTS.

1. If anyone despises the decision of the judges appointed by us, let him pay six solidi to the judges, let the amount of the fine be twelve solidi, and finally, let him lose the case.

2. If indeed, the judges appointed by us render decisions unjustly, let them know that a fine of three times twelve solidi must be paid by them to us without question.

---

[1] For *aut equis animalibus,* Beyerle substitutes *aut aequis animalibus,* i.e., "or similar animals." Cf. Beyerle, *op. cit.,* p. 116, n. 1.

XCI

OF FREEMEN WHO COMMIT A THEFT WITH A SLAVE.[1]

If a native freeman commits a theft with a slave, we order that the sheep, goat, pig, or beehive which was stolen be compounded threefold according to the value established by us; indeed, let the slave receive three hundred blows, and let nothing be sought from the master of the slave.

XCII

OF WOMEN WHOSE HAIR HAS BEEN CUT OFF IN THEIR OWN COURTYARD.[1]

1. If any native freeman presumes to cut off the hair of a native freewoman in her courtyard, we order that he pay thirty solidi to the woman, and let the fine be twelve solidi.

2. But if the woman has gone forth from her courtyard to fight, and her hair has been cut off or she has received wounds, let it be her fault because she has gone forth from her home; and let nothing be sought from him who struck her or cut her hair.

3. If he has done this to a maidservant in her courtyard, let him pay six solidi to the maidservant, and let the fine be two solidi.

4. If a slave presumes to do this to a native freewoman, let him be handed over to death and let nothing be sought from the master of the slave.

5. But if the master of the slave wishes to redeem him from death, we order that he redeem the slave with ten solidi.

6. Also we order that after the slave has been handed over to the master by the judge, let him receive a hundred blows, so that afterward he will do injury to no one nor bring loss to his master.

[1] Cf. LXX, 1.

[1] Cf. XXXIII.

XCIII

OF ARMS AND LEGS WHICH ARE BROKEN BY ANOTHER.

If anyone has broken the arm or leg of another with a stone, stick, or with the back of an ax, we order that he pay fifteen solidi to him; and let the fine be six solidi.

XCIV

OF SHIPS.

1. If anyone presumes to take a ship or a boat, let him pay twelve solidi to him to whom the ship belongs, and let the fine be four solidi. Indeed, for the boat, let him pay four solidi, and let the fine be two solidi.

2. If a slave has done this, let him receive two hundred blows for the ship; for the boat let him receive a hundred blows, and let nothing be sought from the master of the slave.

XCV

OF TRACKERS (*Vegii, Veiatores*).[1]

If anyone has lost a bondservant, a horse, ox, cow, mare, sheep, pig, bees, or goat, and if there is a way-pointer (tracker, *vegius*) present (who helps him), let him pay the way-pointer five solidi for the bondservant; for the horse, three solidi; for the mare, two solidi; for the ox, two solidi; for the cow, one solidus; for the sheep, one solidus; for the pig, one solidus; for the bees, one solidus; for the goat, a tremissis.

XCVI

OF GUARANTORS (OATHTAKERS).

If anyone, either Burgundian or Roman, undertakes to be a guarantor (oathtaker), and if the property of his wife has been offered as surety for the pledged debt or for any debt of the husband himself, let the guarantor (oathtaker) suffer no loss for the

[1] Cf. XVI, 3.

lge, but only on the condition that the husband for whose debt property of the wife has been pledged absolve himself as a guarantor (oathtaker), and restore the property of his wife which has been pledged.

XCVII

Of Hounds (*Canes Veltravi*), Hunting Dogs (*Segutii*), or Running Dogs (*Petrunculi*).[1]

If anyone shall presume to steal a hound, or a hunting dog, or a running dog, we order that he be compelled to kiss the posterior of that dog publicly in the presence (*in conventu*) of all the people, or let him be compelled to pay five solidi to him whose dog he took, and a fine of two solidi.

XCVIII

Of Falcons.

If anyone presumes to steal another's falcon, either let the falcon eat six ounces of meat from his breast (*super testones*),[1] or if he does not wish, let him be compelled to pay six solidi to the owner of the falcon; moreover, let the fine be two solidi.

---

[1] These are specialized terms applied to various types of hunting dogs and are very difficult to translate because of their obscure nature as descriptive terms. For *canes veltravi* (*veltris, veltrahus*) which seems to mean some kind of hound, cf. DuCange, *op. cit.*, II, 95. For *segutii* (*segusius, seugius, seucis*) which means a dog which follows the spoor (*Latihunt* or *spurihunt*), cf. *ibid.*, II, 95. For *petrunculi* (*petronius*) which means some kind of dog with heavy pads on its feet so that it can run across stones or rough ground, cf. *ibid.*, II, 95.

---

[1] There is a good deal of dispute about the expression *super testones*. That given here, "from his breast," seems most generally accepted. For various other interpretations of this law, cf. Davoud-Oghlou, *op. cit.*, I, 414, n. 1; and also cf. Jacob Grimm, *Deutsche Rechts-Alterthümer*, p. 690. Another suggestion has been made by J. Battista of the Rice Institute, that *testones* might be an augmentative form of *testa*, "head," and might mean something like the modern Italian *testuna*, "big head." Thus the law might suggest that the falcon be allowed to eat the meat from (placed upon?) the thief's head.

XCIX

Of Sales Which Are Made Without Witnesses.

1. If anyone has bought a bondservant, or field, or vineyard, or landsite and house built in any place, we order that if it has not been confirmed in writing or witnessed, he shall lose his payment; that is, provided that the writing has not been subscribed and sealed by seven or five witnesses dwelling in that place.

2. Indeed, if five witnesses are not found to be present, we order that it be signed by three suitable witnesses of blameless reputation from those dwelling in that place; but, if this is not done, we order the document to be invalid.

C

Of Women Who Go to Their Husbands Voluntarily.

If any woman, Burgundian or Roman, gives herself voluntarily in marriage to a husband, we order that the husband have the property of that woman; just as he has power over her, so also over her property and all her possessions.

CI

Of the Marriage Price (*Wittimon*).

1. If any Burgundian of the highest (*optimas*) or middle class (*mediocris*) [1] unites with the daughter of another (probably of the same class) without her father's consent, we order that such a noble make a triple payment of one hundred fifty solidi to the father whose daughter he took, if he took her without stating his

[1] Here again the text seems faulty. As it stands the law seems to rank the highest and middle classes together into an upper class as opposed to the lower class or the *leudes*. The difficulty is that the wergeld quoted is that of a *mediocris persona*, according to II, 2. However, the wergeld of the lowest class here called *leudes* (in II, 2, called *minores personae*) also differs from forty-five to seventy-five solidi. Beyerle substitutes a text which would read: "If any Burgundian noble unites with the daughter of another noble without her father's consent, we order that noble, whoever he may be, to make a triple payment of one hundred fifty solidi to the father with whose daughter he united without declaring his intentions or seeking his consent." Cf. Beyerle, *op. cit.*, p. 126, and DeSalis, *op. cit.*, p. 114.

intentions in advance or seeking his consent; and let the fine be thirty-six solidi.

2. Indeed if one of the lower class (*leudes*) has presumed to do this (i.e., has married one of his own class without her father's consent), let him likewise make a triple payment, that is, forty-five solidi; and let the fine be twelve solidi.

CII

OF JEWS WHO PRESUME TO RAISE THEIR HANDS AGAINST A CHRISTIAN.

1. If any Jew presumes to raise a hand against a Christian with fist, shoe, club, whip, or stone, or has seized his hair, let him be condemned to the loss of a hand.

2. But if he wishes to redeem his hand, we order him to redeem it with seventy-five solidi; and let the fine be twelve solidi.

3. Besides this, we order that if he has presumed to raise a hand against a priest, let him be handed over to death, and let his property be given into our treasury.

CIII

OF VINEYARDS.

1. If anyone presumes to enter another's vineyard by day for the purpose of theft, let him pay three solidi to the owner of the vineyard, and let the amount of the fine be two solidi.

2. If he has presumed to do this by night, and has been struck so that he dies, let the guardian of the vineyard suffer no blame.

3. But if a slave has done this, having entered stealthily by day, let him receive three hundred blows.

4. But if he has entered by night, let him be killed just as we have stated above.

5. But if his master wishes to redeem him, he may have that power, provided that after he has redeemed him, the slave shall receive one hundred fifty blows, so that neither he nor the slave of any other may take delight in doing such things.

6. Also, if the native freeman has not been seen (in the act), but

afterward has been found either through a way-pointer (tracker, *vegius*) or by search, we order that he be compelled to pay twelve solidi to the owner of the vineyard to redeem himself, and let the fine be six solidi.

CIV

OF ASSES.

If anyone presumes to hold another's ass without the consent of its owner, and drives it for his own errands (*in ambascia sua minare*),[1] for one or two days we order that he return the ass and another like it to the owner.

CV

IF ANYONE HAS TAKEN ANOTHER'S OXEN IN PLEDGE.

We have found this under title one hundred five in the law of Constantine: if anyone presumes to take in pledge another's oxen, let him be punished capitally. This is resolved by us and our nobles that whoever has another's livestock and has presumed to take in pledge such bondservants, or horses, or cattle, shall lose his case. If he has presumed to take in pledge two oxen, let him pay twelve solidi to him whose oxen he took; and if he has taken in pledge two pair, twenty-four solidi, and let the fine be twelve solidi; nevertheless, under this condition, that he return the cattle to the owner.

[1] Cf. DuCange, *op. cit.*, I, 219.

CONSTITUTIONES EXTRAVAGANTES

ADDITIONAL ENACTMENTS

(Titles I–XVII repeat Titles LXXXIX–CV of the Code above)

XVIII

This Should Be Observed with Respect to Vineyards.

1. The complaints of many Burgundians and Romans have come to us stating that their vineyards have been destroyed by animals, pigs, as well as other beasts; after discussing the matter thoroughly with our nobles (*obtimates*), we have perceived that it is just, and so it seems just to us, that if animals shall be found in a vineyard by anyone, he should have the full power of killing one from the herd of pigs and applying it to his own use.

2. And if it fittingly pertains to the welfare and peace of all, let a similar condition hold in the case of other animals and livestock, with the exception of oxen and horses, as in the case of pigs.

XIX

Of the Arrest of the Guilty.

1. Gundobad, king of the Burgundians, to all his counts.

From statements made by many, we know that horse thieves and housebreakers have resorted to such madness that they commit crimes and all evil not only secretly but also publicly. And therefore we give this precept to you, that if you are able to find those horse thieves or housebreakers, open criminals as well as suspects, do not delay to seize them and bring them before you immediately; with the further provision that if he who has been seized and brought before you can prove himself innocent, let him depart a free man with all his property, and let him not presume to bring an accusation on account of the fact that he has been bound and seized.

2. But if he has been found guilty, let him receive the torments of the death penalty which he deserves, and let his property be taken by those who seized him.

3. And not only is it permitted to pursue a criminal in the district (*pagus*) where he lives, but also, as the common welfare and safety require of everyone, let him not hesitate to seize persons of this sort in other places belonging to us (under our jurisdiction), and to present them before the judges so that the afore-mentioned crimes may not be allowed to remain unpunished longer.

You will endeavor to bring this our order to the notice of all.

XX

An Edict Concerning Foundlings.[1]

Sigismund, king of the Burgundians.

Since we have learned at the worthy and laudable suggestion of that venerable man Bishop Gimellus that exposed children whom compassion would cause to be taken in are neglected because those who would shelter the foundlings fear that they would be taken from them by legal charges (*calumnians intencio*), and so because of lagging compassion the souls of these children perish wretchedly; wherefore, having been moved by the just suggestion which has been raised in this case by our father of holy memory, we decree by this proclamation and the provisions of the present edict and we state in this declaration of our law that in this matter the rules of the Roman law be observed among Romans and let such litigation as has arisen between Burgundians and Romans be concluded as has been established by us; however those cases of this kind which have been completed before the date of this present edict shall in no wise be changed, and the status of pending business is to be governed by the laws mentioned; establishing however that no one may hereafter dare to impose penalties contrary to this salutary precept.

Given on March 8 (516) in the consulship of Petrus.

---

[1] Cf. *Lex Visigothorum*, IV, 4, 1: *ut pro exposito infantulo ingenuo serviat qui proiecit.*

XXI

HERE BEGINS THE ORDINANCE WHICH OUR MOST GLORIOUS KING
ESTABLISHED AT AMBÉRIEUX IN AN ASSEMBLY OF THE BURGUNDIANS.

1. Since cases of this kind arise within our realm for which no
provision has yet been made by law, we decree by the present
enactment what ought to be observed among our people following
a discussion held with our counts (*comites*).

2. If any freeman is led away into captivity and leaves bondservants within our realm, and if any relative claims or assumes or perchance seeks through our command any such bondservant for
himself, let that captive receive back without protest the bondservant thus supported if he ever returns to his own home.

3. If anyone shall sell his slave or maidservant from our realm into
another land and if the slave thus sold shall return to his original
home after the custom of the country (*more patriae*),[1] we command that he be free; nevertheless with the further provision that
he should know that he will not be held under the tutlage (*patrocinium*) of any other save his former master who sold him.

4. If any free Goth held captive by the Franks shall come into
our realm and wish to dwell there, permission shall not be denied
him.

5. If anyone in time of pillage has lost his slaves and reposing
faith in the enemy (under the protection of the enemy?) has departed with one only as a free woman whom he has set free as a
wife for himself, we order especially that he who freed her may
seek his reward provided that nothing further may be sought from
that woman for such a reason (i.e., perhaps, no payment may be
sought from her).[2]

[1] Beyerle and Binding suggest *amore patriae*, "love of country," as a preferable rendering. Cf. Beyerle, *op. cit.*, p. 134.

[2] The text of this law is also disputed, and does not seem to make much
sense. In the latter part of the law, for *is, qui eam liberavit, mercedes requirere
specialius ordinamus, ut nihil* . . . , Beyerle substitutes *is, qui eam liberavit,
mercedes requiret, et specialius ordinamus, ut nihil* . . . , which he translates
something like: "such a deliverer may seek the reward (for his service as best
he can). And we order especially that that man leave the woman entirely un-
molested." Cf. Beyerle, *op. cit.*, pp. 134–35. However, another possible translation might be: "he who freed her shall seek his reward in vain since we order
especially that nothing further may be sought from that woman for such a
reason."

6. If any person shall come into our realm from another country and shall wish to make his home here, or to dwell with someone, he shall have permission; and no one shall presume to reduce him to servitude through his own efforts or attempt to seek him from us.

7. With respect to different kinds of solidi, we order that all gold of whatsoever weight be received save for four particular issues, namely that of Valencia, the older issue of Geneva, the Gothic money which was coined at the time of Alaric, and that of Adaric.[3] But if anyone will not receive gold of accepted weight save for these four issues of money, let him lose what he wanted to sell without remuneration (i.e., because he would not accept the money [*pretium*] offered).

8. If anyone shall receive a guarantor (oathtaker) and shall presume to take possession of his pledges before he has warned the debtor with whom he had the suit (originally) three times in the presence of witnesses, let him restore the pledges which he presumed to take twofold.

9. If anyone shall buy another's slave from the Franks, let him prove with suitable witnesses how much and what sort of price he paid and when witnesses have been sworn in, they shall make oath in the following manner: "We saw him pay the price in our presence, and he who purchased the slave did not do so through any fraud or connivance with the enemy." And if suitable witnesses shall give oaths in this manner, let him receive back only the price which he paid; and let him not seek back the cost of support and let him return the slave without delay to his former owner.

10. Be it known that whoever attempts to do anything contrary

---

[3] Just what issues of coins are indicated here is not very clear. The first seems to be that minted in the city of Valencia. The second, "the older issue of Geneva," has been suggested to mean coins minted by Gundobad's brother, Godegisil, who shared the rule for a time (474–500) with Gundobad, and who ruled from Geneva. The coins of Alaric would be those of Alaric, ruler of the Visigoths (ca. 390–410), who was reported by the Bishop Avitus to have debased his coins with copper. Upon the meaning of Adaric there is no general agreement. DeSalis cites the possibility of the word's being a corruption of Atalaricianos or Athalaric, ruler of the Ostrogoths (526–34). Beyerle favors its interpretation as Ardaric, a ruler of the Gepedi who had been an ally of the Hun Attila in 451. On the problem generally, cf. DeSalis, *op. cit.*, p. 120, nn. 8, 9, 10, 11; Beyerle, *op. cit.*, p. 137, n. 1.

to this enactment established concerning specific acts must pay by way of fine twelve solidi for each offense.

11. We command this especially, that all counts (*comites*), Burgundian as well as Roman, shall maintain justice in all their decisions; let them avenge and punish severely those who have committed violence, assault, or any crime, so that no one may presume to commit such acts within our realm. Let them judge all cases according to the laws so that the judge may be bound by the ordinance of justice as the law of our ancestors sets forth. For we recognize that this is done openly: you give composition among your relatives for various crimes and the cases are not decided according to the laws; as a result, the people are debased so that they presume to commit similar offenses. If anyone presumes to make composition thus, so that he fails to make judgment in strict accordance with law, let him know that he must pay a fine.

12. We ordain this with respect to Romans, that nothing more may be required by Burgundians who have come among them than that which is prescribed at present, i.e., half the land. Indeed, the other half together with all the slaves may be retained by the Romans, and let them suffer no violence as a result.[4]

13. Furthermore churches and priests must in no wise be held in contempt.

14. If anyone wishes to seek something by way of gift, let him come with letters from his count (*comes*) and let the counsellors (*consiliarii*) or mayors of the palace (*maiores domus*) who are present receive those letters of the count and prepare letters of their own at our command for the guidance of the judge in whose territory (under whose jurisdiction) is found that property which is sought and let the judges grant this to those seeking the gift provided they (the judges) examine into the request with all care and good faith and provided it can be given without injustice.

[4] Cf. LIV.

BIBLIOGRAPHY [1]

EDITIONS OF THE TEXT OF THE "LEGES BURGUNDIONUM"

Leges Burgundionum, edit. L. R. deSalis: *Monumenta Germaniae Historica, Leges, Sectio I*, Tomus II, pars I (Hanover, 1892), 3–122. This is the edition of the text used in the preparation of this translation.

Gesetze der Burgunden, edit. and trans. Franz Beyerle: *Germanenrechte, X* (Weimar, 1936). The translation has been checked against this work.

Lex Burgundionum, edit. Ferdinand Walter: *Corpus Juris Germanici Antiqui*, I (Berlin, 1824), 299–350.

EDITIONS OF RELATED CODES OF EARLY LAW

Codicis Euriciani Leges ex Lege Baiuvariorum Restitutae, edit. K. Zeumer: *M.G.H., Leges, Sectio I*, Tomus I (Hanover and Leipzig, 1902), 1–32.

Edictum Theodorici, edit. F. Bluhme: *M.G.H., Leges, Sectio I*, Tomus V (Hanover, 1875–1879), 145–79.

Edictus Rothari, edit. Ferdinand Walter: *Corpus Juris Germanici Antiqui*, Tomus I (Berlin, 1824), 683–753.

La loi Gombette, edit. J. E. Valentin-Smith, trans. (French) Gaupp and Bluhme, 2nd ed. (Lyons: L. Brun, 1899).

Leges Langobardorum, edit. F. Bluhme: *M.G.H., Leges*, Tomus IV (Hanover, 1868).

Leges Saxonum and *Lex Thuringorum*, edit. K. F. Freiherr von Richthofen: *M.G.H., Leges, Sectio I*, Tomus V (Hanover, 1875–1879), 1–102, 103–144.

Lex Alamannorum, edit. K. Lehmann: *M.G.H., Leges, Sectio I*, Tomus V, pars I (Hanover, 1888).

Lex Baiuvariorum, edit. K. Beyerle (Munich: Hueber, 1926).

[1] This bibliography is not limited solely to works dealing with the Burgundians and the Burgundian law, but contains a few selected titles dealing with the barbarian migrations, feudalism, and medieval law.

Lex Francorum Chamavorum, edit. R. Sohm: *M.G.H., Leges, Sectio I,* Tomus V (Hanover, 1875–1879), 269–88.

Lex Ribuaria, edit. R. Sohm: *M.G.H., Leges, Sectio I,* Tomus V (Hanover, 1875–1879), 185–268.

Lex Romana Visigothorum, edit. Hänel (Leipzig, 1849).

Lex Visigothorum (Forum Judicum), edit. K. Zeumer: *M.G.H., Leges, Sectio I,* Tomus I (Hanover and Leipzig, 1902).

Theodosian Code, edit. Mommsen-Meyer (Berlin, 1905).

Visigothic Code, The (Forum Judicum), trans. and edit. S. P. Scott (Boston: The Boston Book Co., 1910).

EARLY LITERARY SOURCES

Sidonius Apollinaris, *Opera,* edit. C. Luetjohann, *M.G.H., auct. ant.,* Tomus VIII (Berlin, 1887).

Gregory of Tours, *Historia Francorum,* edit. W. Arndt and B. Krusch, *M.G.H., script. rer. Merov.* XIV, Tomus I, pars I (Hanover, 1894).

Prosper Tiro, *Chronicon,* edit. Th. Mommsen, *M.G.H., auct. ant.* IX, (Berlin, 1892), 341–499.

SECONDARY WORKS DEALING WITH EARLY MEDIEVAL LAW

Amira, K. von, *Grundriss des germanischen Rechts,* 3rd ed. (Strassburg, 1913).

Bluhme, F., "Das westburgundisches Reich und Recht," *Jahrbuch des gemeinen deutschen Rechts,* I (1857), 48–89; II (1858), 197–211; V (1862), 207–34.

Boretius, "Ueber Gesetz und Geschichte der Burgunder," *Historische Zeitschrift,* XXI (1869), 1–27.

Brunner, H., *Deutsche Rechtsgeschichte,* 2nd ed., I (Leipzig, 1906).

Cambridge Medieval History: Harold Dexter Hazeltine, "Roman and Canon Law in the Middle Ages," V (London: Cambridge University Press, 1911).

Claparède, H. de, *Les Burgondes jusqu'en 443: contribution à l'histoire externe du droit germanique* (Geneva, 1909).

Daniels, A. von, *Handbuch der deutschen Reichs und Staatenrechtsgeschichte* (1859), I, 154–78.

Davoud-Oghlou, G. A., *Histoire de la législation des anciens Germans,* 2 vols. (Berlin, 1845).

Eichhorn, Karl Friedrich, *Deutsche Staats- und Rechtsgeschichte,* 5th ed., I (Göttingen, 1843).

Esmein, A., *Cours élémentaire d'histoire du droit français,* 11th ed. (Paris, 1912).

Flach, J., *Les origines de l'ancienne France* (1886–1904).

Gaupp, E. T., *Die Germanischen Ansiedlungen und Landtheilungen* (Breslau, 1844), 296–317.

Ginoulhiac, C., "Des recueils de droit Romain dans la Gaule sous la domination des barbares," *Revue historique de droit français et étranger,* II (1856), 529–85.

Glasson, E., *Histoire du droit et des institutions de la France,* II (Paris, 1888).

Grimm, Jacob, *Deutsche Rechts-Alterthümer* (Göttingen, 1828).

Halban-Blumenstock, A. von, *Das römische Recht in den germanischen Volksstaaten,* 3 vols. (Breslau, 1899–1907).

Havet, J., "Des partages des terres entre les Romains et les barbares chez les Burgondes et les Visigoths," *Revue historique,* VI (1878), 87–99.

Hayes, C. J. H., *Introduction to Sources Relating to the Germanic Invasions* (New York: Columbia University Press).

Henderson, E. F., *Select Historical Documents of the Middle Ages* (London, 1892).

His, R., *Geschichte des deutschen Strafrechts bis zur Karolina* (Munich and Berlin, 1928).

Hubé, R. de, "Histoire de la formation de la loi bourguignonne," *Revue historique de droit français et étranger,* XIII (1867), 209–59.

Huebner, R., *A History of Germanic Private Law,* trans. Francis S. Philbrick: *Continental Legal History Series* (Boston, 1918).

Jenks, E., *Law and Politics in the Middle Ages,* 2nd ed. (London, 1913).

Kübler, B., "Zur Sprache der Leges Burgundionum," *Wölfflins Archiv für lateinische Lexikographie,* VIII (1893), 445 ff.

Lear, F. S., "Contractual Allegiance vs. Deferential Allegiance in Visigothic Law," *Illinois Law Review,* XXXIV (1940).

———, "The Public Law of the Ripuarian, Alamannic, and Bavarian Codes," *Medievalia et Humanistica,* Fasc., 2 (1944), 3–27.

Legacy of the Middle Ages, The, edit. C. G. Crump and E. F. Jacob (Oxford: Clarendon, 1926), for articles on "Customary

Law" by Sir Paul Vinogradoff, 287–319, and on "Roman Law" by E. Meynial, 363–99.

McNeal, E. H., *Minores and Mediocres in the Germanic Tribal Laws* (Columbus, Ohio: F. J. Heer, 1905).

Mayer-Homberg, E., *Die fränkischen Völksrechte im Mittelalter*, I (1912).

Pollock, Sir Frederick, and Frederic William Maitland, *The History of English Law before the Time of Edward I*, 2nd ed., I (London: Cambridge University Press, 1923).

Savigny, F. C. von, *Geschichte des römischen Rechts im Mittelalter*, 2nd ed., II (Heidelberg, 1834), 1–36.

Schröder-von Künnsberg, *Lehrbuch der deutschen Rechtsgeschichte*, 6th ed. (Berlin and Leipzig: De Gruyter, 1922).

Stobbe, O., *Geschichte der deutschen Rechtsquellen*, I (Brunswick, 1860).

Strachan-Davidson, J. L., *Problems of the Roman Criminal Law*, 2 vols. (London: Oxford University Press, 1912).

Tardif, A., *Histoire des sources du droit français, Origines romaines* (Paris, 1890).

Taylor, H. O., *The Mediaeval Mind*, 4th ed., II (London: Macmillan, 1930), 260–309.

Vinogradoff, Sir Paul, *Roman Law in Medieval Europe*, 2nd ed. by F. de Zulueta (London: Oxford University Press, 1929).

Viollet, P., *Histoire du droit civil français*, 3rd ed.

Walter, Ferdinand, *Deutsche Rechtsgeschichte*, 2nd ed., I (Bonn, 1845).

Wilda, W., *Geschichte des deutschen Strafrechts*, I (*Das Strafrecht der Germanen*) (Halle, 1842).

Zeumer, K., "Zur Textkritik und Geschichte der Lex Burgundionum," *Neues Archiv der Gesellschaft für ältere deutsche Geschichtskunde*, XXV (1900), 257–90.

Zoepfl, H., *Deutsche Rechtsgeschichte*, II (Brunswick, 1872).

SECONDARY WORKS DEALING WITH THE HISTORY OF THE BURGUNDIANS AND THE BARBARIAN MIGRATIONS

Binding, C., *Das Burgundisch-romanische Königreich von 443 bis 532* (Leipzig, 1868).

Bury, J. B., *History of the Later Roman Empire from the Death of Theodosius to the Death of Justinian*, 2 vols. (London, 1923).

———, *The Invasion of Europe by the Barbarians* (London: Macmillan, 1928).

Calmette, G., *La société féodale*, 2nd ed. (Paris, 1927).

Cambridge Medieval History: Martin Bang, "Expansion of the Teutons," I, 183–217; Ernest Barker, "Italy and the West, 410–476," I, 392–432; Norman H. Baynes, "The Dynasty of Valentinian and Theodosius," I, 218–49; F. G. M. Beck, "Teutonic Conquest of Britain," I, 382–91; Christian Pfister, "Gaul Under the Merovingian Franks," II, 109–32; Ludwig Schmidt, "Attila," I, 360–66 (London: Cambridge University Press, 1911).

Dahn, Felix, *Die Könige der Germanen, Band 11, Die Burgunden* (Leipzig, 1908).

Dawson, Christopher, *The Making of Europe* (London: Sheed and Ward, 1932).

Dickins, Bruce, *Runic and Heroic Poems of the Old Teutonic Peoples* (London: Cambridge University Press, 1915).

Dill, Sir Samuel, *Roman Society in Gaul in the Merovingian Age* (London: Macmillan, 1926).

———, *Roman Society in the Last Century of the Western Empire*, 2nd ed., rev. (London: Macmillan, 1925).

DuCange, *Glossarium Mediae et Infimae Latinitatis*, 7 vols. (Paris, 1842).

Fliche, A., *La Chrétienté médiévale, 395–1254* (Vol. VII, Pt. 2 of Cavaignac, *Histoire du Monde*), (Paris, 1929).

Freeman, E. A., *Western Europe in the Fifth Century: An Aftermath* (London, 1904).

Fustel de Coulanges, *Histoire des institutions politiques de l'ancienne France*, Vol. II (*L'invasion germanique et la fin de l'Empire*), 5th ed., 1924; Vol. III (*La Monarchie franque*), 5th ed. (Paris: Hachette, 1926).

Gibbon, Edward, *Decline and Fall of the Roman Empire*, edit. Bury, 4th ed., IV (London, 1911).

Gregory of Tours, *The History of the Franks*, translation and introduction by O. M. Dalton, 2 vols. (London: Oxford University Press, 1927).

Guilhiermoz, P., *Essai sur l'origine de la noblesse en France au moyen âge* (Paris, 1902).

Gummere, F. B., *Germanic Origins* (1892).

Halphen, L., *Les Barbares* (Vol. V in *Peuples et Civilizations*, edit. Halphen and Sagnac), 2nd rev. ed. (Paris, 1930).

Hodgkin, T., *Italy and Her Invaders*, III (London: Oxford University Press, 1896).

Jahn, A., *Geschichte der Burgundionen, und Burgundiens bis zum Ende der I Dynastie*, 2 vols. (Halle, 1874).

Jullian, C., *Histoire de la Gaule*, VII–VIII (Paris, 1926).

Lamprecht, K., *Etudes sur l'état économique de la France pendant la première partie du moyen âge*, French trans. by Marignan (Paris, 1889).

Lavisse, Ernest, *Histoire de France*, II (Paris, 1911).

Léotard, E., *Essai sur la condition des barbares établis dans l'empire romain au IVe siècle* (Paris, 1873).

Lot, Ferdinand, *The End of Antiquity and the Beginning of the Middle Ages*, trans. P. and M. Leon (New York: Knopf, 1931).

———, *Les invasions germaniques* (Paris: Payot, 1935).

Moss, H. St. L. B., *The Birth of the Middle Ages, 395–814* (London: Oxford University Press, 1935).

Odegaard, C. E., *Vassi and Fideles in the Carolingian Empire* (Cambridge: Harvard University Press, 1945).

Oman, Sir Charles, *The Dark Ages, 476–918*, 6th ed. (London: Rivington, 1914).

Petrie, W. M. F., "Migrations," *Journal of the Anthropological Institute*, XXXVI (1906), 189 ff.

Pirenne, H., *Mohammed and Charlemagne*, trans. B. Miall (New York: Norton, 1939).

Previté-Orton, C. W., *Outlines of Medieval History*, 2nd ed. (London: Cambridge University Press, 1929).

Saleilles, Raymond, "De l'établissement des Burgondes sur les domaines des Gallo-Romains," *Revue bourguignonne de l'enseignement supérieur*, I, 43–103.

Schmidt, L., *Geschichte der deutschen Stämme bis zum Ausgang der Völkerwanderung*, I–II (Berlin, 1910–18). (Vol. I, 2nd ed. rev., Munich, 1934).

Stephenson, C., *Mediaeval Feudalism* (Ithaca: Cornell University Press, 1942).

Stevens, C. E., *Sidonius Apollinaris and His Age* (London: Oxford University Press, 1933).

Thompson, James W., *An Economic and Social History of the Middle Ages* (New York: Century, 1928).

Villari, P., *The Barbarian Invasions of Italy*, trans. Linda Villari, 2 vols. (London, 1902).

Waitz, G., *Deutsche Verfassungsgeschichte*, 3rd ed., II (Berlin, 1882).

Wietersheim, E. von, *Geschichte der Völkerwanderung*, 2nd ed. by F. Dahn, 2 vols. (Leipzig, 1880–1881).

INDEX

University of Pennsylvania Press
MIDDLE AGES SERIES
Edward Peters, General Editor

Katherine Fischer Drew, trans. *The Laws of the Salian Franks.* 1991

Katherine Fischer Drew, trans. *The Lombard Laws.* 1973

Robert D. Fulk. *A History of Old English Meter.* 1992

Nancy Edwards. *The Archaeology of Early Medieval Ireland.* 1990

Margaret J. Ehrhart. *The Judgment of the Trojan Prince Paris in Medieval Literature.* 1987

Richard K. Emmerson and Ronald B. Herzman. *The Apocalyptic Imagination in Medieval Literature.* 1992

Felipe Fernández-Armesto. *Before Columbus: Exploration and Colonization from the Mediterranean to the Atlantic, 1229–1492.* 1987

Patrick J. Geary. *Aristocracy in Provence: The Rhône Basin at the Dawn of the Carolingian Age.* 1985

Peter Heath. *Allegory and Philosophy in Avicenna (Ibn Sînâ), with a Translation of the Book of the Prophet Muhammad's Ascent to Heaven.* 1992

J. N. Hillgarth, ed. *Christianity and Paganism, 350–750: The Conversion of Western Europe.* 1986

Richard C. Hoffmann. *Land, Liberties, and Lordship in a Late Medieval Countryside: Agrarian Structures and Change in the Duchy of Wrocław.* 1990

Robert Hollander. *Boccaccio's Last Fiction: Il Corbaccio.* 1988

Edward B. Irving, Jr. *Rereading* Beowulf. 1989

C. Stephen Jaeger. *The Origins of Courtliness: Civilizing Trends and the Formation of Courtly Ideals, 939–1210.* 1985

William Chester Jordan. *The French Monarchy and the Jews: From Philip Augustus to the Last Capetians.* 1989

William Chester Jordan. *From Servitude to Freedom: Manumission in the Sénonais in the Thirteenth Century.* 1986

Ellen E. Kittell. *From* Ad Hoc *to Routine: A Case Study in Medieval Bureaucracy.* 1991

Alan C. Kors and Edward Peters, eds. *Witchcraft in Europe, 1100–1700: A Documentary History.* 1972

Barbara M. Kreutz. *Before the Normans: Southern Italy in the Ninth and Tenth Centuries.* 1992

E. Ann Matter. *The Voice of My Beloved: The Song of Songs in Western Medieval Christianity.* 1990

María Rosa Menocal. *The Arabic Role in Medieval Literary History.* 1987

A. J. Minnis. *Medieval Theory of Authorship.* 1988

Lawrence Nees. *A Tainted Mantle: Hercules and the Classical Tradition at the Carolingian Court.* 1991

Lynn H. Nelson, trans. *The Chronicle of San Juan de la Peña: A Fourteenth-Century Official History of the Crown of Aragon.* 1991

Charlotte A. Newman. *The Anglo-Norman Nobility in the Reign of Henry I: The Second Generation.* 1988

Joseph F. O'Callaghan. *The Cortes of Castile-León, 1188–1350.* 1989

William D. Paden, ed. *The Voice of the Trobairitz: Perspectives on the Women Troubadours.* 1989

Edward Peters. *The Magician, the Witch, and the Law.* 1982

Edward Peters, ed. *Christian Society and the Crusades, 1198–1229:* Sources in Translation, including The Capture of Damietta by Oliver of Paderborn. 1971

Edward Peters, ed. *The First Crusade:* The Chronicle of Fulcher of Chartres *and Other Source Materials.* 1971

Edward Peters, ed. *Heresy and Authority in Medieval Europe.* 1980

James M. Powell. *Albertanus of Brescia: The Pursuit of Happiness in the Early Thirteenth Century.* 1992

James M. Powell. *Anatomy of a Crusade, 1213–1221.* 1986

Michael Resler, trans. Erec *by Hartmann von Aue.* 1987

Pierre Riché (Michael Idomir Allen, trans.). *The Carolingians: A Family Who Forged Europe.* 1993

Pierre Riché (Jo Ann McNamara, trans.). *Daily Life in the World of Charlemagne.* 1978

Jonathan Riley-Smith. *The First Crusade and the Idea of Crusading.* 1986

Joel T. Rosenthal. *Patriarchy and Families of Privilege in Fifteenth-Century England.* 1991

Steven D. Sargent, ed. and trans. *On the Threshold of Exact Science: Selected Writings of Anneliese Maier on Late Medieval Natural Philosophy.* 1982

Sarah Stanbury. *Seeing the* Gawain-*Poet: Description and the Act of Perception.* 1992

Thomas C. Stillinger. *The Song of Troilus: Lyric Authority in the Medieval Book.* 1992

Susan Mosher Stuard. *A State of Deference: Ragusa/Dubrovnik in the Medieval Centuries.* 1992

Susan Mosher Stuard, ed. *Women in Medieval History and Historiography.* 1987

Susan Mosher Stuard, ed. *Women in Medieval Society.* 1976

Jonathan Sumption. *The Hundred Years War: Trial by Battle.* 1992

Ronald E. Surtz. *The Guitar of God: Gender, Power, and Authority in the Visionary World of Mother Juana de la Cruz (1481–1534).* 1990

Patricia Terry, trans. *Poems of the Elder Edda.* 1990

Hugh M. Thomas. *Vassals, Heiresses, Crusaders and Thugs: The Gentry of Angevin Yorkshire, 1154–1216.* 1993

Frank Tobin. *Meister Eckhart: Thought and Language.* 1986

Ralph V. Turner. *Men Raised from the Dust: Administrative Service and Upward Mobility in Angevin England.* 1988

Harry Turtledove, trans. *The* Chronicle *of Theophanes: An English Translation of* Anni Mundi *6095–6305 (A.D. 602–813).* 1982

Mary F. Wack. *Lovesickness in the Middle Ages: The* Viaticum *and Its Commentaries.* 1990

Benedicta Ward. *Miracles and the Medieval Mind: Theory, Record, and Event, 1000–1215.* 1982

Suzanne Fonay Wemple. *Women in Frankish Society: Marriage and the Cloister, 500–900.* 1981